NUMBERS – THE MASTER KEY

BY

CLAYNE CONINGS

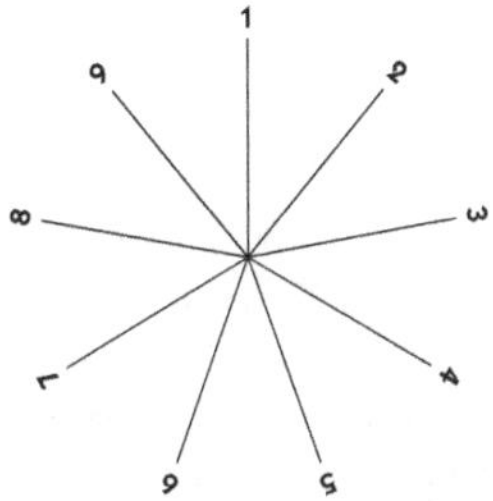

Is Your Name Balanced?

Inherent within your
life experiences
lie great possibilities.

Are you taking from
them all that you can?

NUMBERS –
THE MASTER KEY

by Clayne Conings

An Imprint of:
1st World Library
809 S. 2nd St.
Fairfield, IA 52556

ISBN: 1-887472-94-0
LCCN: 2002115307

Graphic Designer:
Sharon A. Dunn

Contact:
Clayne Conings
guiding@intergate.ca
604/299-2337

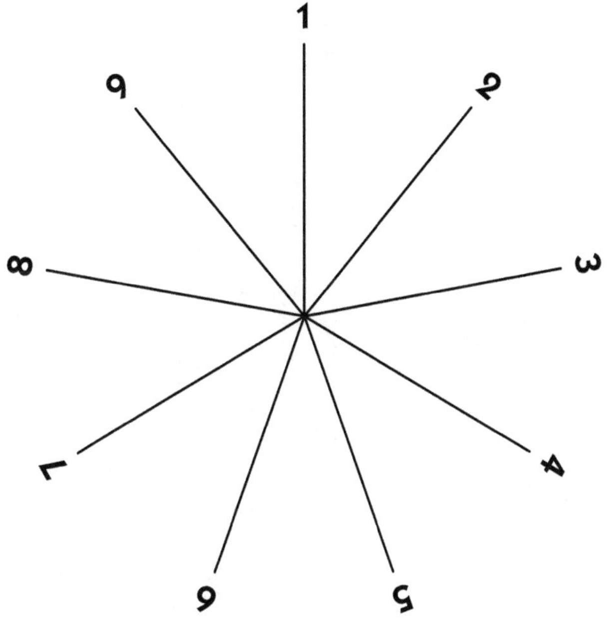

1
2
3
4
5
6
7
8
9

Contents

Introduction:
Evolution of Spirit through Mind – The Author's Explanation of the Essence of the Book 1

Chapter 1:
Symptoms versus the Root Cause – A Criticism of the Current Methods of Dealing with the Problems of the Mind 7
Working out Your Name 39
Three Basic Character Types or Groups 47

Chapter 2:
Spiritual Evolution through Numbers 55
One 59
Two 81
Three 94
Four 109
Five 117
Six 132
Seven 149
Eight 165
Nine 184

Chapter 3:
Sample Analysis of Marlon Brando 207
In Conclusion 218
Application for a Personal Analysis of Your Name 255

INTRODUCTION:

The Evolution of Spirit through Mind – The Author's Explanation of the Essence of the Book

Life is both a mystery and a vast expanse for exploration and exquisite pleasure. The earth is filled with beauty. Our senses are designed to respond to all that life is. Individually, that amounts to the sum total of what we have put into our mind. Therefore, it is to the mind that we must go to understand how to open to life, as it is reflected through our senses.

Life is to be found where the masses do not believe it exists. It is a great treasure that requires a map. The magnificence of it can be felt and perceived in consequence of our every thought. Life grows as the mind expands through concept and time, and it all begins with the right or *whole name.*

One person may look out onto a beautiful view and not feel or register much of anything, while another will be awed and overwhelmed by its beauty. We may experience deep pleasure and a profound communion while in conversation with someone because of what is spoken, or we may forget in an instant that we ever spent a moment together because nothing significant occurred. It is all a product of our mind!

If the *name* is not correct the mind will not respond to all that life offers, but will become short-suited and limited to specific interests. In time the mind unwittingly violates the *whole* and suffers accordingly.

In the deepest sense we are all complete, or the essence of our very spirit is all-inclusive, but its expression or release is dependent upon its vehicle, the mind. The mind and character grows or doesn't grow as it moves through life's experiences. We respond to an experience according to the nature of the mind and its inherent qualities as created through its association with language and our *name*.

Spirit or the forces of reason can only express as human consciousness through language when identified through a *name*. Why we all respond differently to the same or similar experience has always been a mystery to all but those who understand how mind or consciousness comes into being in the first place. If the *name* is incomplete in its numerical or mathematical structure the mind fails to respond to all that life could be. Inherent within all life's experiences there is a mystery to be solved or lessons to be learned. The complete mind that is balanced to its spiritual nature will extract or comprehend the potential beauty within an experience, while the incomplete mind will invariably develop a rationale to support its own escape from a situation that registers too much pain or difficulty.

It is only when we bring forth all that we are, and could be, that the senses respond to the divine spark which is life individualized. So we must simply sort out that which is real from that which is illusion. Individualization is a process of personal discovery that can eventually bring forth the spirit or reason of our life through our contribution, but only if that contribution is consistent with the evolutionary movement of truth, reason and logic. The only thing that evolves or expands is reason or consciousness of life. Change in itself seldom produces growth.

There are nine expressions of spirit or the life force. It is through numbers and their relationship to letters and one's name that we are able to separate each aspect or quality of a person's character to see how they function and deal with their life's experiences. If there is not a harmony or balance of these nine forces within the name, then the individual will become dysfunctional. In this state the mind becomes trapped into chasing its problems, and becomes a prisoner of them.

The spirit or universal reason of life is attempting to express or evolve that which it is. It does so through the finite plane as human consciousness, but only to the degree that the minds of men and women can comprehend the theory or plan of life and their individual relation to it. It is not so much a consciousness of the outer world of form that should be our focus. It should be with our thoughts and their relationship to our inner life that should be of concern.

Mental growth or an expansion of mind then, depends upon the study of these nine aspects of reason as they express through human experience, individually and collectively. These nine qualities, when combined to form character and personality, represent powerful lessons. This wisdom, through the ages has almost disappeared through ignorance of the principles regarding the creation of human mind.

A balanced name given to a child from birth is the most sacred and important act of a parent. This provides the child with the potential to move through life adapting and then extracting the lessons inherent within their experiences. If the child's name lacks the components from which to draw, then the mind will move away from many of its opportunities for growth and favor only its limited field of interest. It then unwittingly violates its whole nature and in due course becomes dysfunctional. How to reconcile these sometimes-contradictory elements of our character into a single whole is the mystery that has been kept secret or just simply lost. It is referred to as the Master Key.

The obvious retrogression and degeneration of life reflects the failure of humanity to learn its lessons. The rise and fall of civilizations and of individuals testifies to the incompleteness of the growth cycle. A premature collapse or decline of a society, or of an individual, suggests an imperfection, a fatal fault or omission in the plan or perception of life in its completeness.

It is the intention in the writing of this book to illustrate the fundamental steps leading to a spiritual individuality. We were born to be free men and women. That is, free from the constraints within ourselves and within our societies that limit our creativity and our enjoyment of life. Freedom is acquired by virtue of our creativity, intelligence and the nature of our contribution.

The promise of life is in experiencing the pure joy of it! There is a power behind mind as it expresses through a current of sound in the form of wisdom. It is through the spoken word that all of our lessons lie and our purpose is revealed.

– CLAYNE CONINGS

CHAPTER ONE:

Symptoms versus the Root Cause – A Criticism of the Current Methods of Dealing with the Problems of the Mind

The complexity of modern life has obscured its simplicity. Education, intending to create freedom, has produced conformity. Organized religion, whose purpose is to expand our consciousness of life, has a questionable history and leaves us suspicious and doubtful of its intentions. Science, after taking us out of the dark ages, has created the illusion through technology that we are now living in an advanced state of human evolution. Business, having the power to distribute the goods of the earth equitably for the benefit of all, is without a conscience and is therefore blind to its own destructiveness. Politicians have become a source of ridicule, and the political arena the last place that the wise see as a standard for integrity, trust and dynamic change. Governments wield enormous power, but contain little wisdom and are almost completely ineffectual in changing the mental state of the masses. Art has in the past been used to inspire and ennoble the mind with visions of human potential, beauty and greatness, and has now been reduced to a medium for self-expression and madness.

Reason

In theory life should not be so difficult to understand. The force behind life represents the intelligence in and of life. It is an evolutionary force moving through time, and pushing humanity forward as it expresses itself through human consciousness and human endeavor. It seems that only a few are aware of this movement. The secret to happiness and well-being is simply to align ourselves with the intelligence of life through our actions and our accomplishments. This force only evolves as we expand our consciousness of a personal destiny, as we pursue our interests in the many walks of life, and through a commitment to self-improvement and a dedication to serve life itself.

In trying to understand life it is essential to arrive at the fundamental conclusion that all of existence has reason or a purpose for being. We may not know or believe that a particular thing has a reason for being, but not knowing this does not mean that a reason does not exist. The very fact that something does exist implies or even proves that a reason, although hidden, also exists. If we take a handful of seeds we may not know their purpose or reason until we put them into the soil and watch them produce the flower, if that is the case. We could not see the flower within the seed but it was there nonetheless, waiting for a chance to unfold. If the seed is an annual for example, and does not produce the flower then the plant simply dies and is forever gone. If the seed reaches fruition, which is the reason of its being, then we also see the production of the new seeds which allow for expansion and continuation.

So it is with whole cultures, or as individuals we too must reach a flowering of our efforts in order to produce meaning, destiny, truth or soul quality. If we do not evolve or come to a flowering, a culture or an individual will go into a slow decline because the life or spirit essence is forced to withdraw. Through time and history we observe the inevitable collapse of a culture or of an individual. It is pitiable to watch old people grasping for life and hanging on with no chance to go forward. There obviously is some slow spiritual evolution taking place collectively and individually, but it seems that only a few produce a flowering or wisdom, in a single lifetime, sufficient to produce a soul that will expand and perpetuate itself through others.

We each have a purpose or reason for our being. Just look at the difference between people and their qualities, inclinations, natural talents and temperaments. This implies a different path, lessons to learn, or a different meaning or reason for our existence. Getting caught in the fierce struggle to survive, the purpose can easily become obscured. Throughout time, the great souls of the earth all arrive at the same conclusion that self-knowledge, self-realization or God (reason) realization is what life is all about. Unfortunately, this has been related to the practice of meditation and the belief that silence and a still mind can by itself lead to spiritual awareness or a realization of the reason of our being. That is foolish.

There is work to be done and a great process to understand before there is any impression felt from the source of our life. To quote the Gnostic Gospel of Thomas, "If you bring forth all that is within you, then all that you bring forth will give you life. If you do not bring forth all that is within you, then that which you do not bring forth will destroy you."

In the Christian sense, "Seek first the kingdom of heaven within and all things shall be added unto thee," implies the same thing. The things that are "added" to us come in consequence of our focus on our purpose "first." Today, our fears demand our first attention and take us away from our true purpose. Few people can make a distinction between the call to serve God (reason) or mammon. Until the mind has opened up to the creative impulse it will be motivated by a thousand different fears and will be turned away from the 'kingdom of heaven within.'

The mass of humanity blindly goes out to work at jobs that are barely tolerable because they feel they must. They would say they have no choice. They fear the consequence of doing that which they love, and that which could furnish meaning to their existence. We have become so responsive to our physical needs that we have lost sight of those needs which could make us happy. Fear, due to the absence of money is a strong motivation, forcing us into a system that is fraught with tension and sickness. We have been educated to it. Worry has become a way of life, and an integral part of the system we live in.

It has become so bad that we feel guilty if we are not busy with our worrisome responsibilities.

If there is any spiritual movement in life, it is the product of the few courageous souls who attend to their own business first, and whose passion for life dwells inherently in their desire to serve life, and not themselves exclusively. These few awaken the creative urge and a sense of their purpose.

These few are not so concerned with the daily struggle of providing for their basic needs, but are motivated by a sense of their purpose and the human destiny. Only they enter into a life beyond the obsessiveness of worry.

All problems are directly or indirectly related to a lack of insight into one's purpose. An indifference or lack of interest in the meaning of, and the sacredness of life, will automatically pull the mind down to a preoccupation with its problems. If the mind has not reached the creative state it is pulled into a problematic condition and is consumed, as if by a cancer. That is the way it works when it is tied too much to the emotional plane or the life of self-concern and self-pity. Giving to life reverses that process.

Sense Dependence

There should be no mystery about the human function. Man/woman is mind but only to the extent that we learn to use it as an instrument of perception and conception. For most of us it is impossible to use the mind as a creative force, for the purpose of becoming aware of our reason for life. Why? Because the useless things we fill our mind with have become preoccupations. We have a choice but can no longer exercise that choice because we have become sense dependent. Where there is no wisdom early in life, selfishness or an ego begins to develop that needs to be fed, and the eternal struggle between good and evil begins. At this point the ego working through the emotional plane seeks emotional stimulation and needs to be entertained. It seeks to listen to music rather that create it. It wants to buy paintings rather than produce them. It desires to read books rather than write them. It lives vicariously on the creativity of others believing itself to be cultured, and gathers knowledge and appears wise but seldom has an original thought of its own.

If the mind has not experienced the joy of accomplishment it usually seeks sense stimulation and becomes dependent on it. If the individual mind drops too low it becomes 'problematic' or focuses on problems and fails to discover that it unconsciously perpetuates them. Eventually this 'problematic' condition infects the whole society and demands attention. In response we build institutions that cater to and perpetuate human misery where a few become wealthy trying to cure the symptoms of ignorance, and then they construct theories that lead to a maze of complicated psychological mental gymnastics that further bog the mind down in states of self-pity. Soon, without knowing it, we have lost the joy of living.

The popular view is to travel in reverse and attempt to release the repressed emotions stemming from an earlier trauma in our dysfunctional past. I recently watched a man relate to an audience his story of sexual abuse by his mother when he was a very young boy. He looked to be around fifty years of age. He claimed to have been in therapy for at least ten years. As he began his testimonial he became overwhelmed with emotion and tears, and as he continued his story he became more 'choked up.' He created enormous sympathy and moved the audience to tears. The idea left was that there are elements deep within the psyche that are repressed and responsible for the person's present state of unhappiness, and that they must be released. These elements are supposedly traceable to an early experience, so as he gets in touch with his 'feelings' and 'owns' the problem there is supposed to be a release and a healing that takes place. Presumably this man has been crying for ten years. What a waste! While living in an emotional state we will unconsciously or deliberately look for something to cry about without realizing that we are perpetuating that emotional state. These people will never, ever, find real happiness until they have dug themselves out of the 'pit' of self-pity.

In pacifying the ego there is the danger of strengthening it and perpetuating the problematic state. The gamble here is that in the expression of the agony the therapist will search out the cause and lead you out of the problem. I say this humbly, that only God, or the very wise know where the true source of the problem lies. Believing that the root cause is linked to our dysfunctional background is truly only dealing with the symptoms.

Take for example, the physician who makes the discovery that the gall bladder is diseased and is the basic cause of the problem, but never asks why the organ is diseased in the first place, and believes that removing the organ is the final solution. So, the therapist can be led to believe that an early experience has created a block or a problem that the patient refuses to deal with. He then leads the patient back to that experience hoping somehow to release the block. The problem here is that the therapist assumes that the early experience is the basic or root cause of the problem. This is absolutely not so. What they do not know is why one child responds to an experience and produces a phobia and another child subjected to the same experience is spared a similar reaction.

Modern-day psychiatry, like modern-day physicians, are profoundly aware of the symptoms of disease, both physically and mentally. They must be given credit for their contributions, but because they have so little understanding of the human mind itself, they avoid too much reference to the true source of all problems, as originating in the very structure of the mind. All problems originate in the mind first, through imbalance, and that imbalance reacts to an experience to create a block or phobia. It must be remembered that the phobia is only a symptom.

The point here is that we may play around with the symptoms of anger, lack of confidence, fear, shyness, repression, hate and jealousy, and trace them back to a childhood experience, but there is no guarantee that the patient will move beyond their influence when they are recalled. The patient's mind being prone to reacting to an experience in a specific way, is likely to continue creating new phobias throughout their life as a consequence of the nature of their mind. If the therapist has any success over the patient it is only because the therapist is a living example of the wisdom of life in its entirety, and the patient has sufficient intelligence and receptivity to truth to be helped in the first place, for only wisdom can lead the mind out of the maze of ignorance.

In my work I have met a number of people influenced strongly by the 'new age' concepts of 'owning' your problems or 'getting in touch with your feelings.' There was a resentment in these people if I suggested that they should attempt to exercise some control over their moods, angers or depressions. Their idea was that the moment they felt the mood or anger coming on they must not resist it, for in the resistance the mood would create even more of a problem through its suppression. They believed that the mood was an integral part of themselves and must be 'owned' or acknowledged as such.

The mood is actually an interference, a creation of the mind or ego, that can in time be dissolved through confronting it as it shows itself in our endeavor to achieve our goals. They insisted that I was not being honest, that I was suppressing my feelings, that I was hiding from something, and that I must get in touch with my feelings by displays of emotion, and that I should cry more often or I was not being honest.

Common sense dictates that sooner or later the mind must recognize its potential to become master of its thoughts and exercise control over its moods etc., or through habit the mood takes over completely. The mood will not go away by itself. We may analyze a presumed cause going back in time, or even see its destructiveness, hoping that we can establish control through willing it out of existence. It is only through time and wisdom and coming to know our purpose in life that we replace the negative emotions, such as moods or anger, with energy and happiness. The mood then dissolves of itself because we are no longer giving it life through 'owning' it. In due time the mind becomes so strong that it recognizes immediately when an interference such as a mood is registering itself through the emotions or nervous system, and it can then 'will' it away.

The danger inherent in the present psychology is that there may be the illusion of healing because the patient's ego is being soothed into believing that everything is alright now. Finally they are being supported and understood in their misery and it feels good. They have finally found a shoulder to cry on and to tell their miserable story to, and it feels so good. Subtly, the selfish orientation or self-pitying state is being perpetuated and in truth the therapist and the patient are living a lie. The ego has won the contest and the patient can continue to live in the state of mental inertia. The patient is unaware that they only feel good in the presence of the therapist who supports them in their misery.

Self-healing and self-worth takes place through accomplishment and giving into life. We should not accept the theory that we are suppressing our emotions, that our sexual fantasies, our anger, or any intense feeling must be expressed or the repression will create problems in our health and in our psyche. So again, it is not the emotions, but wisdom itself that is being suppressed! If we choose to give expression to our negative emotions and frustrations we may experience relief afterwards but the problem is not solved and the chasm between wisdom and insanity becomes wider. The suppression theory is an excuse used by those who have continually failed in exercising self-control.

Spiritual Insight

Only if the mind has sufficient courage and strength will it choose to confront the 'phantom' or the ego directly. If the mind can endure the effects of the 'phantom,' as it registers itself through the body and nervous system as fear, depression, or doubt, it will emerge victorious to become aware of its own power. It is when the mind moves beyond distortion and the problematic state, that impressions from the source or reason of one's life begin to be felt, and register as a thought or a spiritual insight. This does not occur when the mind is still preoccupied with the incidentals of living, but when the mind is truly creative and living beyond a sense-dependent existence. The problematic plane suggests the existence of a wounded ego, that like a wounded and ferocious animal, will fight to the death in its attempt to survive.

Surrender to spirit and not the ego, is the process of surrendering to reason by the gradual development of the mind. Our life and every thought we think becomes our prayer. Nothing is more satisfying than *feeling* the reason of your being reflected through your thoughts, giving to you a sense of direction and a purpose for living.

Wisdom is the Principal Thing

Let it be said that those who are passing through or have passed through the initiation and have mastered even to a small degree the control of the senses, will have discovered a level of peace and stability that was worth the effort. They will live apart from the masses and will invariably be accused of lack of feeling or even of suppressing their emotions. In truth, these people will have removed the distortions of concept that cloud the mind, and will have freed the senses so that the higher vibrations of thought and feeling can be experienced. Love is the result. Love of all life. These ideas are not new but are alien to those who are in the midst of the struggle and cannot yet choose or recognize the difference between feeding the ego and resisting the temptation to do so.

Emotionalism has within itself a tendency for self-perpetuation. As they say "misery loves company," particularly its own. Self-pity is the curse of mankind, blinding the mind and compelling it to analyze itself and its problematic state ad infinitum. It is because of many of these theories that another theory has emerged denouncing the 'mind' itself as something that gets in the way and must therefore be put aside so that some great spiritual force might emerge. "Get out of the head and into the heart" is the statement made by those who seem never to have experienced the true joy of thinking. Those whose mental or emotional confusion is self-perpetuating have never been able to make a distinction between a truly creative mind and one that is always worrying about things. It seems to me that many of these odd ideas develop to justify and support lazy minds, or arise out of sympathy to the almost irreversible confusion of the masses, catering to their problematic state and allowing them to wallow in their own misery. When we cannot succeed at conquering our addictions we invariably develop a rationale to support and perpetuate, and even justify the addiction. This crazy state has given rise to a legion of medical professionals who take your money and listen to your problems and give the illusion through sympathy that you are being cured.

Be careful in soothing the ego or the hurt, as a way of avoiding a hard lesson. The actual truth of the 'new age' idea of 'owning' your problem is that the problem ends up owning you. Only wisdom brings clarity.

Speaking of wisdom and the wise; they cannot be sympathetic to your problems, only to the source of your creativity. You cannot bring your problems to the 'Guru,' only your heart and soul. Then and only then can there be compassion and instruction.

Life calls individuals to ultimately bring forth their wisdom, through creativity, discovery and service. We are no different than any other part of the animate world, but being the conscious part we do not respond to the reason of our being instinctively. We are compelled to think and inquire as to the way of life and to discover the spirit or reason of our life through our creative accomplishments, but this can occur only if we are motivated by a spiritual ideal.

Objectivity

Problems are solved through mental objectivity. In fact, problems are a condition of the emotions created through the mind. As it has been said, a problem cannot be solved on the level of the problematic state itself. All problems are created through lack of spiritual fulfillment. We blame, we get angry, get in a mood, cry, feel self-pity, all because we are found wanting for that happiness that comes through our creativity. The artist at work is totally free and happy, and at that moment has mental objectivity. They are above their problems for the moment. Even if they choose to consider a personal problem, they see it in the light of their inspiration and may wonder what the fuss was all about. If they allow themselves to drop from that state, their mind gets pulled back into *feeling* the problem. A problem may exist in the mind of one person but may not be there in someone else, purely by virtue of what we call objectivity. In one sense we all have problems, but to the objective mind a problem is merely something to solve, while to the emotional person it becomes something to worry about. For the majority, the cause or reason for problems is an imagined one and this self-deception obscures the truth. The solution lies in dissolving the black, heavy force that draws the mind into itself and its own problematic state. This black force grows as the mind unconsciously caters to its own egotism.

The point here is objectivity. I have heard it said that we cannot move forward in life until we have cleaned up our past, that the past is holding us back. That is not quite true. It would be more appropriate to say that we cannot clean up the past until we go forward. In other words, creative accomplishment moves the mind to a higher level of consciousness, and while problems still have to be solved, we reach a point where most problems, being a creation of the ego, have dissolved with the ego. In the immature, lower or emotional state we can love a person one moment and hate them the next. While we are drawing from the higher we cannot be affected by the negative mental plane. Worry and confusion give power to problems while creativity closes the channel, allowing them to die for lack of expression. Have you noticed that when you feel angry there is a compulsive urge to express that anger? If you had the power to suppress that anger long enough to consider its consequences, in time your mind would discover a great power within itself. We must ultimately free ourselves from the urge to hurt, and instead, awaken the spirit of kindness. It is all a matter of concept.

We have all met a chronic complainer who sees a problem in everything and everyone. A million lifetimes would not be sufficient time to solve their problems because they would only create more. As we alter our state of consciousness, through our activities in creative endeavor, we find that there is no need to go back into our dysfunctional past to regurgitate and relive our abused childhood. If there is any value in being brought back into our past, it is only because the facilitator has sufficient knowledge to use a person's bad experiences as a contrast to the beauty and wisdom of life itself, for wisdom is the principal thing.

A large number of people will remain in limbo, their lives revolving forever around their problems as they are pulled into the vortex of confusion by the force of their self-pity. If they could come to a place of power and wisdom – sufficient to stand firm in the midst of their self-pity – and see how they were feeding their problem and their ego, they may then also discover the very essence of their being which brings enlightenment to all of life's dilemmas.

Mental growth or spiritual unfoldment is dependent upon and related to a person's accomplishment. What is growth but the assimilation of knowledge pertaining to life and one's personal destiny? This takes place as we acquire talents and abilities in our endeavor to succeed. While it may require more effort to take lessons on the piano than pour out our problems to our therapist, if we persist with the piano the opportunity for self-inquiry is limitless as we learn to persevere. The effectiveness of a therapist is equal only to their degree of wisdom. The mind fluctuates between pessimism and optimism, between worry and happiness, all because of the state of vitality of the body and the bloodstream. It has been said that one of life's greatest secrets is in the understanding of how to maintain and conserve the vital force within the body. Mood changes correspond exactly to the state of vitality of the body. Stress, worry and the indulgence in excitement of an emotional nature quickly deplete the vital force so that one day we feel happy and the next we wake up grumpy, and few really understand why this is. The mind can only maintain positivity through achieving mental and emotional maturity through understanding life in its entirety. So it is to the mind that we must look to understand the reasons why the body suffers its momentary depletions of vitality. More of this will be explained later.

Language

What is the point of life and what is this thing called Wisdom? Human life represents the medium of consciousness and reflects the life current, reason, or very cause of existence. Without consciousness there is seemingly no point to life. A bear for instance, has no interest or curiosity to discover the meaning of life, but merely responds to life instinctively and performs its function according to the nature of its species. If a bear is around a million years from now it will still be doing the same thing it has always done, while we humans have the potential to evolve or expand our consciousness from a lower state of awareness to a higher one. In the Christian sense we are the eyes, ears and mouthpiece of God the source. It is as if God the source creates man and woman (or mind) in its own image as the final act of creation. In a sense the creative essence or God manifests itself in the finite plane in the form of mind, language or consciousness.

And so "In the beginning was the Word, the Word was with God, and the Word was God." In one sense there really is no beginning, but with the advent of the word or language we have the dawning of consciousness. (Language being synonymous with man/woman.) There is no life except in thought through language.

There is a mystery here that has been hidden from the masses for centuries; a key that promises to release the mind from its confusion. The wisdom in these sayings has been deliberately hidden in its simplicity and its profundity. The seeker is being drawn to inquire into the mystery hidden within language and the *power of the word*. Not just in the meaning of the *word* as it relates to quantity of thought but also as it relates to quality or power. This force is released through sound as it expresses through wisdom.

Thinking

All of life is revealed through consciousness or thought. We cannot stop our thoughts. Thinking is synonymous with mind, consciousness and the human species. All human achievement and advancement has been a process of bringing the unknown to the known, the unconscious to the conscious, the unmanifest to the manifest. It all happens through thinking.

There is an idea prevalent that in order to access the higher or spiritual force we must first stop thinking. The object is to create a void where the mind cannot interfere so that the spiritual force can emerge from that emptiness. There are techniques designed to focus the mind through concentrating on an object or on something that eventually blocks out the incessant mental 'chatter,' and this supposedly makes way for enlightenment. This whole concept is putting the cart before the horse. Let me assure you that nothing can come out of the void but that which is relative to what you put into it in the first place. We can only access thought relative to where we are in our present awareness.

It is the process of learning to think constructively and clearly that eventually awakens the spiritual force. We truly only stop the 'chatter' when we learn to direct our thoughts towards meaningful pursuits. The exercise here is to discriminate between useless thought impressions and creative ones. Refinement of thoughts, habits, conduct and attitudes, along with a strong sense of purpose, eventually produces a strong mind capable of stopping the useless 'chatter.'

We can never stop the mind from receiving thoughts but we can succeed in curbing its creative potential by putting it to sleep from lack of use. A peaceful and harmonious mind is a product of *right thinking* and not the result of the cessation of thought. Mind is meant to wander, it moves at random and touches on material or thought impulses that are relative to an individual's focus. If there is no power or focus in the mind then that mind becomes impressionable and is literally taken over by useless thoughts.

Thinking is our greatest asset and a source of inspiration and eventually our means of enlightenment. We feel and experience the spiritual force as we learn to think in a spiritual and loving way.

Religion

All religions have been created with one predominant theme, which is to explore our relationship to God the Principle or Cause. Religions attempt to satisfy the soul's quest for union with a Creator in various ways. Adherents of religions of the West and the Middle East are encouraged to enter into devotion, prayer and acceptance of a divine personality, and are provided instruction through a Holy Book as to the best way to conduct one's life. In the East, the theme is much the same but with an additional emphasis on meditation. Both share a common idea in the concept of 'surrender.' The idea is that at some point in our religious practices it is possible to experience a spontaneous act of surrender which unites us to our creative source. In the East, Yoga has the meaning of *union* between the mind and its inner consciousness. Religions universally then have the responsibility to instruct humanity in the ways of surrender. It is fair and honest to say that religions experience small success in this matter, that is, if we are to take this idea of surrender to its deepest meaning.

Surrender

The concept of 'surrender' could be taken to mean surrender 'up' something such as the ego, or surrender into something such as a higher spiritual state. My explanation encompasses both ideas. Before any level of surrender can take place there must be a sacrifice of the 'self' before the spontaneous act of union is experienced on any level.

What is important to realize is that the act of surrender is more of an active process than a passive one, a moving towards one state from a prior one. In other words, a person may pray or meditate for an eternity and achieve almost nothing.

The *spirit* of anything lies within the thing itself and must be approached through intelligence and hard work. Let me explain. If you choose to awaken the *spirit* of music within piano playing, you will not discover it through passively sitting there waiting for something to happen. It is after ten or more years of diligent study and practice that the intuitive faculty begins to awaken automatically and the fingers finally move across the keyboard effortlessly, and only then does the *spirit* of the music begin to emerge. Of course you realize that it is *your* spirit that begins to emerge through your achievement. Finally you are ready to perform or give yourself to your audience. If you have done your work you will inspire the audience and the audience applauds because you have brought spirit into the atmosphere. If you are wise and feel your power, you bow in humility and gratitude, not to the audience but to your very source or spirit. In other words, nothing comes from nothing. Therefore it follows that surrender into the *spirit* of the music is hardly a passive act. And so it is with the spirit that presides in all of life. It reveals itself only when our mind encompasses all of life, or at least the vital parts of life. In other words the mind must become as big as spirit itself if there is going to be any union!

It is important to note that the *intuitive* element within the mind awakens automatically as it grows through its achievements. There is a certainty or truth *felt* but only after reaching towards a certain level of completion in our endeavor. Intuition is a product of wisdom and wisdom is the result of mental and intellectual development. Let us not be naive and believe that it is better to rely on our intuition rather than our mind. Remember, our mind receives on the level of its output. We may chuckle at the computer terminology 'garbage in, garbage out' but that, in a rather coarse way, is a fact of life. Enlightenment or happiness is not accessible to the superficial or fatalistic mind.

Fatalism

A very long time ago religion fell prey to the disease of 'fatalism.' The dictionary meaning of fatalism is quoted as: " The doctrine that all events are ordered by the arbitrary decrees of God." This has left us in a state of confusion, fear and subservience to the 'genii that rule the earth.' We have been forced to our knees, praying for our 'deliverance' from our own ignorance. Fatalism is not merely a religious phenomenon but has crept into almost every segment of our society.

Western religious fatalism suggests that alone, we cannot solve our problems. We may create them but we cannot solve them without the help of God. Divine intervention then, becomes the solution and a substitute for our failing mind. The solution is promised through a system of devotion and prayer, and yielding to a higher power. Two thousand years of practice seems not to have delivered us from our confused state.

Eastern religious tradition suggests much the same, that you cannot do it by yourself. Here we must find the `enlightened' one and until there is surrender to the 'living master' there cannot be any spiritual transformation. In my own observation, the millions of devotees of this system do not become enlightened through their association with the Guru. What is the problem?

Because the efforts by millions to solve their day-to-day problems meet with such little success, it becomes obvious why fatalism is so popular. We cry out for help, we curse our Gods, we prostrate ourselves in despair. We are considered saved if we are 'born again' into a religious revival where our morality may be altered somewhat, but not too much else has changed.

Giving oneself to the concepts of fatalism is giving oneself to emotionalism. Fatalism breeds despair through false hope, anticipation of reward without effort, and feelings of futility engendered through self-pity. Faith in God then, resigns us to believe that we must learn to accept our infirmities because God has 'decreed.' While it is true that most people cannot change substantially, the real truth is that they have never been taught how.

We have given our 'power' away because of fatalism. We look to governments, politicians, institutions and professionals to solve our problems. The whole system caters to and perpetuates the 'problematic' state.

Growth by Law

Nothing comes from nothing. The power, the plan and the law of growth of a seed is within the seed. When the seed is planted and watered the law is invoked and the growth begins. Not one step in the growth of the plant that began with the seed can be altered or missed. Everything is subject to growth by law. Only in this sense is everything 'ordered by decree.'

"When God breathed into man the breath of life he became a living soul." When the child takes its first breath you might say that God the reason becomes involved in form or the physical body, and becomes subject at that point to the laws governing His own growth. God becomes individualized and separate from the whole or source, and is therefore subject to the laws relative to species. The only difference between the plant and the human is that the human must travel the road or the 'law' consciously. There can be no divine intervention or transgression of the 'law.' God the reason, becomes involved in form or species and becomes subject to the law governing that life form. If we violate the laws of right living through ignorance we must and will pay the price. Ignorance is no excuse, and prayer or meditation could only serve to stimulate reason but not solve the problem in itself. For example, over-indulgence in sugars and sweets will eventually produce a physical reaction that no amount of praying will alleviate.

Life is a duality or a product of a principle of cause and effect. Reason is contained within form and the growth of that form is governed by that reason.

It is easy to see how 'mind' in its undeveloped state gives in to fatalism when it cannot solve its problems, or where reason has been replaced by emotionalism.

In the preceding pages I have implied the existence of a knowledge or process that applies to all people. Growth of mind takes place through reaching out for concepts to explain the meaning and basic cause to all human problems. There are nine lessons or perceptions that relate to human evolution. They are difficult to learn. Inherent within each lesson is a great power that is needed in the effort to learn the others.

The Process

We now come to the process. While the path of life differs from person to person the lessons are the same. We may take the path of business, science, art or some particular trade, and if we are to advance in one of those fields, and in our life, the lessons of patience, perseverance, leadership, kindness and other lessons must be learned. Mental growth or spiritual unfoldment is really a matter of building character. When the ego or 'phantoms' appear to try to stop us from succeeding, the mind has a chance to master their negative influence. If we give in to them, and giving in becomes a habit, the mind becomes 'problematic.' If we master the lessons involved in our endeavor the mind becomes strong, resilient, responsible, aware and ultimately wise. Our abilities grow with our successes.

There is one very important point here to consider and that is 'intent.' Whether we learn much from our projects or our work is entirely based upon our motives or our intent or reason for doing them. While our growth is dependent on our accomplishment, the effort must be linked to an ideal or a thought of giving, serving or adding some worth to the sum of human progress. Otherwise an 'ego' begins to grow and interferes with the mind's ability to analyze a problem fairly and objectively. If the motive is too much for 'self,' the building of a business for instance can still grow by the force of one's personality and ego but there is little development of substance and character, and the business will continually suffer from the individual's character deficiencies.

After the talents and abilities of the individual have reached a certain point, and the endeavor has become spiritually motivated, a sense of meaning and satisfaction begins to be felt and a purposefulness becomes apparent.

Evolution

Over a large span of time it is easy to see an evolutionary process taking place in nature and in all of life.

So it is with the forces of reason as they express through human mind and an expanding consciousness. There is an intelligence and a process involved here. There is a rhythm or a spirit in life that is attempting to express and evolve. An individual mind can merge or tune into this universal urge. This rhythm can be accessed when we choose to work for the expansion of life. When our motivation for work benefits life, and our relationships awaken the urge to help and serve each other, then we will eventually experience the joy of creative thought and its inspiration.

My effort from this point will be an attempt to outline this process; to clarify and explain the meaning, reason or wisdom of the individual as they learn their lessons on the path of life. But first a little theory.

A Theory

First of all I ask you to be open, for the moment, to the theory that the forces of life, consciousness or mind can be defined or separated into nine component parts. This diverse expression of human characteristics in a single personality can be understood by applying mathematics or numbers to language and time. Language provides the basis for conscious expression, and mathematics or numbers provides the means that allow the separation of the conscious force into its nine component parts. The function of mind is to serve as the vehicle for the evolutionary force of reason and to allow it to manifest that which it is. What we are going to study is the evolutionary force itself.

The human mind is linked to reason, or the evolutionary force, through language and our name. If a child is not named there will be no consciousness. It is vital to name a new-born child immediately after birth, or very soon thereafter. How well the child adapts to the changing circumstances of life is determined by the correlation of the conscious forces as they are related to the name given at birth. The underlying principle deals with the concept of a *balanced name.* It is not my intention to explain this theory in this book, but only to suggest that the forces of consciousness can be defined through applying mathematics to language. The theory is thoroughly explained in class work and available to anyone who cares to study this profound principle.

A Little History

This knowledge appears in virtually all the great religions of the world, albeit in fragments. Pythagoras the Greek philosopher was supposedly initiated into this secret knowledge in his travels through Egypt. My research reveals that the Semitic peoples of the Middle East were introduced to this secret through Egyptian sources. As well, it appears independently in the Far East, as well as in other parts of the world.

In southern France during the middle ages, Jewish scholars were clever enough in the study of their Holy Books to realize they were on to something. Their fascination with the Torah and other writings revealed and suggested a profound mystery contained in the study of the relationship between numbers and letters. A few of these Jewish scholars had been exposed to a great secret, which if understood, promised to reveal the mystery of life itself. Numbers or simple mathematics in relation to the letters of any alphabet came to be revered as the 'Pathway to God.' Subsequently, the Jews established schools to study this knowledge in southern France under the safe haven set up by the Christian Cathars. These concepts were developed and written down in a form which came to be known as 'Kabalah.' Eventually the 'safe haven' was removed by the Catholic crusaders who decimated the Cathars, and the knowledge of Kabalah once again went underground. It showed up in the mythological literature of the Grail Romances and the Holy Grail, and later appeared in the writings of the Free Masons under the mystical idea of 'The Lost Word.' In recent times the knowledge has reappeared in a system called Numerology, no doubt influenced by the earlier Kabalistic teachings. There were some serious efforts to understand the practical value of these ancient ideas up until about 1940, then numerology veered off into a world of fantasy.

What is revealed in this ancient wisdom is indeed the pathway to God.

The Pathway to God

We define this knowledge as a pathway to God because it clearly demonstrates the lessons that must be learned if we are to become wise to the way of life. Those of us who have studied this work, have a tool or a point of reference when confronting our problems or challenges from day to day. We do not have to become tangled up in complex psychological theories. We can perceive and relate our problems to an imbalance within the qualities of our character. The problem of dysfunction is not abuse in itself but is the mind's response to that abuse. With one mind the individual may have the power to resist responding negatively, or they may eventually outgrow the effects of abusive parents for example. Another mind may attempt to armor itself against abuse and subsequently develop some strange phobia or fear. So the dysfunction is a symptom, not the cause of a problem. The cause lies in the unbalanced mind of the individual. This is clearly revealed in class work. Most of us unconsciously try to escape from our problems through some form of illogical rationale, and this of course will result in a distorted perspective of the situation. With the knowledge of the mathematical principle we know exactly the reason for our resistance to a problem. We have the key that allows for mental objectivity, or an unbiased look at the problem and at ourselves.

The mind is made up of nine distinct qualities. Like sound in a musical scale, there exists a principle or law of harmonics. When these nine qualities are brought together through language and our name they create our overall personality. When they are not harmonized or balanced they can produce extremes, such as too much or too little sensitivity, or perhaps the insatiable and uncontrollable urge to talk with little interest in what others have to say, or a scientific bent where the mind is limited to a microscopic view of life, or to the extremes of idealism that make it impossible to deal with the realities of everyday life. Then there are the reclusive types and a myriad of other extremes of character. Present-day theories have never explained this distorted image or flaw in the human psyche. Modern psychology is bewildered as to why therapy or psychoanalysis fails, in most cases, to bring a person back from the realms of mental imbalance. The imbalance is inherent in the name and eventually recorded in the genetic make-up.

The gene again is only a symptom. Tampering with genes will never solve the problem of disease whether it is physical or mental. Medical science must not delude itself into believing it is on the threshold of removing illness from the human race because it thinks the genetic element is the root of the problem. Medical researchers must ask themselves this question: Why does the gene that records a susceptibility to cancer for example suddenly appear? Where does it come from in the first place? Why does it have the capacity to appear, disappear and reappear in families through the generations? A gene is a small living particle that responds to the influences of the quality of mind and lifestyle. Mind is either evolutionary or degenerative, and the body responds and records accordingly.

In the following pages I will attempt to explain the division of the life energy or reason manifesting as consciousness in its 'nine' distinct vibrations or qualities. So that you may be able to more easily relate to these qualities, here is the way that you calculate the predominant influences affecting *you* through *your* name and birthdate.

WORKING OUT YOUR NAME

1	2	3	4	5	6	7	8	9
A	B	C	D	E	F	G	H	I
J	K	L	M	N	O	P	Q	R
S	T	U	V	W	X	Y	Z	

Looking at the above key chart you will note that each letter has a numerical equivalent, in that A,J,S have the value of '1;' B,K,T have the value of '2;' and so on.

Now for example, let us work out the name Robert:

	6		5		
R	**O**	**B**	**E**	**R**	**T**
9		2		9	2

We begin by making a distinction between the vowels and consonants by placing the numerical value of each vowel above the letter, while we place the numerical value of each consonant below the letter, as shown above.

Now we simply add up the vowels separately: 6+5=11. Then reduce 11 into a single digit by adding 1+1=2. The 2 then becomes the sum total of the vowels in the name of Robert. We do the same with the consonants: 9+2+9+2=22. Then reducing 22 to a single digit we add 2+2=4. The 4 becomes the sum total of the consonants.

Finally add the total of the vowels 2 plus the total of the consonants 4 equals 6. It looks like this:

	6		5			= **2 soul**
R	**O**	**B**	**E**	**R**	**T**	
9		2		9	2	= **4**

Then 2+4 = 6 or 2-4-6

= **6 expression**

The numerical combination for the name of Robert is a 2-4-6 combination.

Always remember to reduce the totals to a single digit. In the name of Robert the only numbers that are analyzed are the soul number which is 2 and the expression number of 6.

Let's try again with the name, Harold:

	1		6			= **7 soul**
H	**A**	**R**	**O**	**L**	**D**	
8		9		3	4	= **6**
						= **4 expression**

It is the 7 and 4 that are analyzed in the name of Harold.

The following is a sample name analysis of those names that share the 7-6-4. The following analysis then is a product of the combined influences of the soul number of 7, with the expression number of 4. Remember that all 7-6-4s will not be identical because of the influences of the surname, the combined names and the birthdate qualities.

Thomas – Harold – Joan – Carol –
Angela – Sonia – Jacob – Meaghan
7-6-4

These types are painstakingly detailed, proficient and patient. Concentration, orderliness and a focus on the finer points of a job are their main characteristics. These people are the analysts, scientists and workers who deal best with mathematics, computers, mechanics or anything which requires attention to detail. They have the patience and the power to finish the things they start. Theirs is the life of steady, systematic and slow progress. Change can be very disturbing because it upsets the routine. They live by routine. This is a quality that lives by the adage, "Show me, I'm from Missouri." Their minds work on the basis of fact and within the realm of the five senses. They are not particularly theoretical or open to philosophical speculations. Things have to have the stamp of approval by academia or the scientific community before they will accept and follow a train of thought. They must see and understand from the basis of their own experience before an idea will register in their consciousness as a truth. These people are naturally skeptical and slow to change. They are traditionalists who will not question the status quo. Their love of detail can awaken an ingenuity and patience that can see them accomplish things that others would give up in frustration. It is this patient inquiry and seeing a job well done that is the source of their inspiration. Their minds are meticulous in covering all the details and putting things in exactly the right place. This is the quality of research and science, with a profound aptitude for discovering a truth through mathematics and form. Confidence is not their strong point. They are afraid to step out and try something new. Familiar ways are the safest path for them. They are reliable and hard-working. Their resistance to change can be a sore point in their relationship with others. They would rather be left alone to pursue their hobbies than deal with pressing personal and social problems. Their speech is slow, deliberate and thoughtful, and while everyone else has moved on to other topics, they are still pondering the previous idea. The men generally find an outlet through mathematics, mechanics, accounting and the various trades. The women often end up in dead-end jobs, pushing paper around, generally being frustrated in life. They can both become bogged down in the small things for lack of vision, incentive and drive. As it has been said, they cannot see the forest for the trees. They are inventive if they are left alone uninterrupted, but become discontent if pushed or if they must work by deadlines. Their homes are a place of solace and comfort where they can putter around in their gardens and kitchens pursuing their personal interests. When these people are unbalanced, the tension in their lives will affect them through stomach and intestinal disorders. Constipation is the main problem area as well a weakness in the heart lungs and bronchial organs.

For a further study of how the number qualities relate to all names I would advise you to refer to my book **Miracle of Names**.

Exception to the Rule

In the name of Lynn for example, where there are no vowels, the Y becomes the vowel. If the name is spelled Lynne then the Y becomes a consonant. Only when there are no other vowels in the name does the Y become a vowel.

The surname which is a lesser influence can also be worked out. Then there are the influences of any nicknames to be worked out. The amount of influence of any name is determined by the amount of use.

Now to determine the influence which we call your birth path, we must work out or apply numbers to your time of birth.

Example:

Taking the birth date of Nov. 12 1957. November is the 11th month, so let us reduce 11 to the single digit of 1+1=2. Then the 12th day is reduced to 1+2= 3. Then the year 1+9+5+7=22 and 2+2=4 then adding 2 from Nov. 3 from the 12th day and 4 from 1957. 2+3+ 4=9

It looks like this: Nov. 12, 1957

2 + 3 + 4 = 9

The 2 influence lasts from birth to 27 years, the 3 from 27 to 54 and the 4 from 54 to the end of life. The 9 is the major influence and is felt throughout life. The 2, 3 and 4 are minor influences.

Before we can become *Masters* of living and life, in control of our destinies, we must respond consciously to the spiritual urge. We must answer the call from within through thought and action by becoming conscious of the inherent lesson of each number.

Now with the numbers that you have worked out as the main influences in your life you should be able to relate to their meaning as you read their description and their lesson.

Even though no number or quality is better that any other number or quality there is a progression or evolutionary progress from 1 through 9. Each quality or number is integral to the whole and depends upon all of the others numbers for a full expression of itself. The life force or spiritual nature of all people is identical and contains all that life is, but it expresses differently according to the relationship of one number to another. The challenge we all have is to reconcile one aspect or quality of our life with another.

Before I explain or define each quality and the lesson that each represents, it is important to learn and remember some basic points:

First Point

All life and mathematics or numbers are based upon a principle of **thirds**. While there are nine expressions of the life force, and nine being divisible by three, you will find if you study this work, that there are three basic character types or three basic life lessons. A person's character type is determined by their *day* of birth.

Second Point

The Number qualities 1, 2 and 3 represent the **first third** and relate to the steps or lessons dealing with 'self' and the struggle to acquire for 'self' that which will satisfy its physical, emotional and personal needs in the highest possible sense.

The qualities 4, 5 and 6 deal with the lessons relating to analysis, mental discrimination, logic and truth. In other words, if there is no clear reasoning ability the spirit force within will be suppressed. Even though all life is theory, mental evolution through science, music, religion or any other aspect of human endeavor is entirely dependent upon the mind's ability to conceive actual LAW. These forces must be understood as they relate to the phenomenon of equilibrium, or how they correlate with each other. There is no standing still in nature, we either evolve or we produce a condition of mental stagnation which leads to collapse or disintegration. We may hold to any theory that satisfies our preferences but if it is not consistent with truth we will simply not progress. We must be scrupulously honest and have a point of reference that is large and all-encompassing before the mind can move itself beyond its self-serving limitations. For example, if the concept of homosexuality is correct and those who practice it are right in their orientation, then they will progress, but if they are unwittingly violating a fundamental law of life, their perception will be a stumbling block in their lives. The 4, 5 and 6 then represent powerful lessons in the development of mental character. The human function is a matter of becoming conscious of the movement of life through time and form. This can only be accomplished through thought. Unmanifest reason evolves into that which it is through language, but only when thought is consistent with truth, which is evolutionary.

The 7, 8 and 9 are difficult lessons and must be learned by all, but their true significance is reserved for the spiritual aspirant. These lessons are approached not so much by personal choice but as a consequence of having reached a degree of self-mastery relating to the 6th stage, the stage of individualization. Then the focus of one's life must go beyond oneself. The entrance to, or the awakening of the spiritual force demands the conquering of 'self' and the perception of the motive force behind every thought and action. If it is exclusively self-serving it is also self-defeating. Entering into the spiritual domain demands that the mind face its phantoms and humble itself in service to humanity. One can no longer enter into the fight with others without first considering the needs and perception of your opponent. Only then will the power behind the WORD be truly understood. Only when the individual mind is ready will it know the time to withdraw from its anger and its judgement of others, and become a silent but powerful influence in others' lives. These lessons are inherent in the deeper understanding of the 7, 8 and 9 quality.

THREE BASIC CHARACTER TYPES OR GROUPS

As you know, the universal intelligence is subject to and understood through the mathematical principle. The principle is based on 9, or 3 x 3. Nine being the complete number has its root in the number three. The principle of thirds is used here to define three basic character types or groups.

Water – Independent

This refers to those people born on a day of a month which is 1, 5 or 7 or a number which reduces to the single digit of 1, 5 or 7. Example: 10, 14, 25 or 28. If you are born on the 28th day of a month then, 28 or 2 + 8 = 1, puts you in the 'Independent' grouping.

These people incorporate the lesson that relates to independence. This is the quality of self-reliance, self-confidence and self-motivation – in other words, it represents the lesson of 'self.' They are not here to work for others. It is their function to awaken their creative and innovative nature as they stand alone, without interference from others. This is a very decisive influence that does not need support from others. They are here to project themselves into life as pioneers, discovering themselves and their talents through their independent creations. It is for them to lead the way through their originality and individual effort. The inspiration of this lesson comes from the power of 'self' as it pushes through obstacles to discover the spark of its own creativity. In association with others this quality does not want to spend a great deal of time discussing personal problems. They do not have the quality of the counselor that easily sits and listens to others' complaints. The more social types would be frustrated in their company because it is projects and ideas that interests them, not dialogue that revolves around people and their problems. If there are problems to be resolved, these types speak directly and to the point. Prolonged discussion about personal problems with people becomes irrelevant and unnecessary. Action and accomplishment are the key-notes here. To be doing things becomes the source of their happiness. They derive a great sense of satisfaction when they can work things out on their own. Only as they learn to stand on their own can they awaken the creative spark and so discover their true nature. Their lesson is to remain unmoved in a crowd or by the crowd, holding their own and speaking only that which arises out of complete self-control.

Fire – Social

This refers to those people born on a day of the month which is 2, 4 or 8 or that reduces to the single digit of 2, 4 or 8, Example: 11, 22 or 26.

This is the social group whose lesson is to respond to the feelings of others with understanding and consideration. It is for them to understand the heart and mind of their fellow beings. They cannot shrug off bad feelings or the results of disagreements very easily. The guilt from personal involvement in any altercation will cling to them until it is resolved. This is their lesson. Outbursts of temper should become the source for their inner inquiry into the deeper meaning of their life. Not until they learn to become the peacemaker can they resolve the mystery of this lesson. Others may dismiss troublesome people with disinterest or indifference, but these people cannot. It is for them to work past the feelings of hurt or disappointment, and discover what is necessary to bring about harmony and friendship. Time and again they will have to deal with their emotional outbursts until they begin to understand the cause of the conflict as it applies to their specific nature. They will carry the residue of their personal conflicts with people until they discover the magic that can be felt when they merge with them in harmony. They are here to counsel, to listen and to make a friend of all people who come into their life. Only as they merge and experience the warmth that nurtures, will they be lifted by the flow of energy that comes with the true understanding of others. They must rise above the urge to discuss and express petty grievances and problems. When they know the difference between sympathy with another's problems, and a sympathy with their higher nature, they will come to know the power in this lesson. As they plumb the depth of another's psyche with patience and tolerance they will have the pleasure of meeting soul to soul. The lesson then, of the 2, 4 and finally the 8 is to reach beyond personality and the fighting, where there is only the urge to be kind.

Air – Inspirational

This refers to those people born on a day of the month which is 3, 6 or 9 or that reduces to the single digit of 3, 6 or 9, Example: 12, 15 or 27.

This group has the lesson of directing emotion to a level of inspiration. Nothing pleases them more than seeing and feeling the response of people to their influence. They are here to perform, to inspire and to motivate others. There is an emotional element at the basis of their character that is to be used to lift people through humor, music or public speaking. They are the most natural entertainers or speakers. Others may teach or deliver their material in a matter-of-fact manner but these people have the power to make their audience cry, laugh or to move them to levels of inspiration and joy. Self-expression is the key-note of their life. When they have overcome 'self' and awakened a certain compassion for others, they will come to know their inner power. This power will express and be felt only as they use their life for the benefit of others. Then they will experience the true essence of inspiration as they see how that influence affects an audience. This power when expressing is charismatic. They have the potential to create a sympathetic link with their listeners, and to feel the power behind emotion or inspiration as it first arises within themselves, and then as it is transmitted to the audience. The result is inspiration. People leave knowing that something has changed or happened because of this power. In this case they have become a conduit for the spiritual essence of life. This is their potential which can be realized only as they understand all that is required in becoming a spiritual teacher. The greatest power of life is felt and experienced as it expresses through sound and the spoken word, as wisdom. This essence moves through their nature and their emotion, but only when it is directed towards uplifting others. Their lesson then lies in understanding the great power hidden in the mystical Word.

It should be understood that all the lessons of the groups are to be learned if we choose to walk the path towards spiritual individuality.

Harmony through Compatibility

In marriage the deepest soul urge can be experienced with those who share the same group quality. People in the water group would do best to marry someone in their own group. Those in the Fire group can merge with either the Water or Air groups, but do better with the Air group (although their own group is preferable). People in the Air group can blend somewhat with the Fire group, but find difficulty with the Water group. The single most important factor leading to a deep understanding with a marriage partner can be found in understanding the group lesson.

It must be remembered that as an individual moves past the elements of personality and into a greater universality of concept they can live with almost anyone. This is the goal for all of us.

Even so, there are those who we will always be able to link with more deeply because of the natural elements of compatibility, particularly as related to the group lessons.

The group lesson is one of the first considerations when choosing a name for a new born child. The many thousands of people who have changed their names through this work will testify to the repression of this group quality if their original name was unbalanced.

CHAPTER TWO

Spiritual Evolution through Numbers

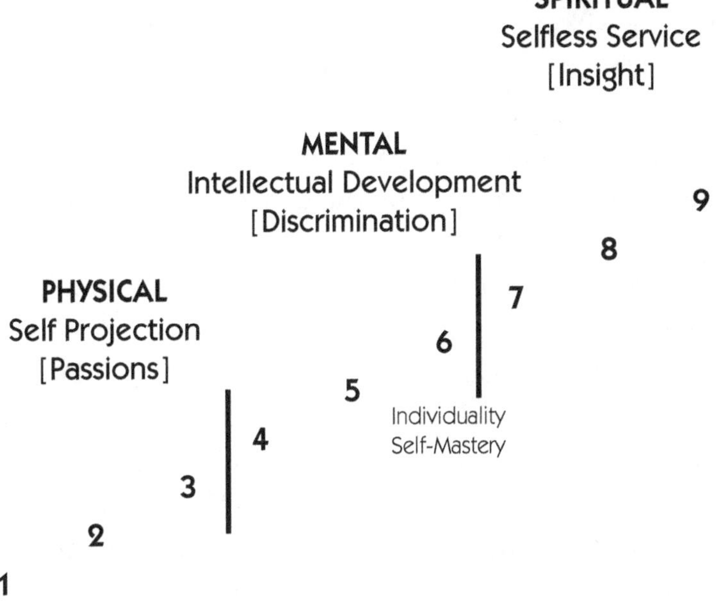

It is the intention of the following discourse to explain as clearly as possible the steps or lessons leading to spiritual progress, at least as much as I am personally able to, according to my own experience and perception. The theory relates to acquiring or incorporating these NINE lessons in order to produce a state of mental equilibrium. Life itself determines when there is enough of each quality learned to allow for an opening of the mind to all that life is, and to its sublime beauty. Only in this state of mental balance will life reveal its mysteries. With each step the senses will open and the mind will automatically respond by degree to what lies behind each lesson. Only in wholeness or balance will the mind reach a level of satisfaction or fulfillment in life, otherwise we will always be found wanting. We must strive to leave life fulfilled. Again I say that the spirit or reason of life expresses only to the degree of our contribution, and our contribution can never be measured by outward effects so much as by our capacity to give through the power of the WORD.

The intention in life is to evolve spiritually by removing the element of 'self' or egotism from our minds so that we can contribute something useful to life. Selfishness invariably appears in every child as it struggles to satisfy its needs and wants. Egotism is the effort of the mind to satisfy its selfish nature. This selfish nature grows and expands when it seeks to satisfy some useless fetish that serves no one but itself. Teaching our children at an early age to be kind, thoughtful of others and creative, reverses the downward spiral of ultimate self-destruction through egotism.

The ego or 'self' expands through obvious and subtle expressions in our everyday life. It is reflected in our poor attitudes towards one another and through our temper and our moods. It expresses through our fears and is kept alive through self-pity. It shows up in religious types through self-righteousness, and even more subtly through those who believe their spiritual practices promise to lead them to some exalted state of enlightenment. Spirit or the reason of life evolves or moves through those few minds who become totally committed to life and its improvement, both personally and collectively.

The life struggle is an exercise in dissolving the negative mental force or ego that has grown through self-serving attitudes, and that pits itself against others and against the progress of the individual and of life itself. Growth and mental power are acquired through understanding the process that leads to ultimately facing the force of this self-destructive and selfish side of our nature. This dark and insidious force operates through the mind, emotions and nervous system of us all. All but the wise can withstand its influence. It has been written about in occult literature and can be recognized by those who approach the threshold to power and enlightenment. The lesson is one of self-sacrifice and service that ultimately leads to a total surrender and dissolution of the 'self ' or ego. It becomes more difficult as the mind moves higher because it requires more endurance and less complaint in the midst of an almost inexplicable mental state. This predicament is encountered again and again by those who are chosen to enter a life of meaning and purpose, until such time as the veil of doubt is removed to make way for greater and greater clarity of purpose. It is the doubting and the possibility of failure, as well as the doubt of our divinity that holds the mind to this dreadful cycle of struggle and reprieve. The following then is an attempt to explain the process that leads the mind to the place where it must stand alone with only a reliance upon its own inner consciousness.

It is well to remind you that without a balanced name it becomes infinitely more difficult to extract the lessons or qualities from our experiences as we move through life.

As you read the following description and lessons of the qualities from 1 through 9, I encourage you to relate these lessons to your own dominant qualities as you have worked them out. This will help you to understand aspects of your character and your life.

ONE

POSITIVE

Independence, Individuality, Originality, Perseverance, Candid, Creative, Physically Strong, Aggressive, Pioneering, Rugged, Hard Worker, Autonomous, Reliable, Honest

NEGATIVE

Self-Centered Materialistic, Coarse & Blunt, Unrefined, Discussion Revolves around Oneself, Not Interested in Others, Egotistical, Skeptical, Domineering, Not Deep Thinkers, Lacking Vision

This is the positive and independent force that is here to contribute something new and original to life. 'Ones' have a singleness of purpose. It is a strong physical force with great perseverance and endurance. The one represents a beginning or a new start with the positivity of carrying it through to completion. They are neither impressionable nor easily influenced and can push their way through obstacles. It represents the lesson of self-projection, where their own interests come before anything or anyone else. They are creative in a practical way and can work well with their hands and their minds. They are blatantly honest and very candid in their verbal expression. When they are unbalanced, they lack tact and diplomacy. In their independence they must be left alone to find their own way in order to be happy and creative. They are very loyal, dependable and hard working. They must strive to become their own boss. As leaders of people they can be a little too domineering and pushy if there is any imbalance. Their innovative and pioneering skills make them the forerunners of achievement. They are ingenious at working things out in an original way. Having great physical stamina they love the outdoors and the ruggedness of nature as well as its solitude. They have very strong opinions and don't mind expressing them and can sometimes offend others without intending to. In itself the 'one' is not particularly sociable nor does it possess great verbal skills. Their task is to project themselves and their ideas forward through action. Sometimes they just cannot find the right words to express themselves, and feel awkward in the company of the more intellectual types. Their self-interest must be watched that it does not lead to a self-serving existence. At times they can be too self-opinionated. It is their self-determination that can at times make them stubborn and skeptical of others' ideas. It is for them to lead the way fearlessly so as to establish their individuality as an inventive and dynamic force. They draw their motivation from the excitement of a new idea and their ability to formulate plans by themselves and in their own way. They must learn not to become too materialistic. When unbalanced this quality suffers from the limitation of measuring others too much from its own point of view. They are not good as debaters or theorists. They tend to see things as black or white with an attitude of 'take it or leave it.' Because of their physical strength, when frustrated, they could sometimes fight rather than back down. In matters of love they are more physical than romantic. They are unemotional with a dry earthy kind of humor. They love to test their strength and their endurance in such things as hiking, running or sports of any kind, or in just plain hard work. They mature quickly as youngsters, and establish their independence faster than most. What few friends they have they are loyal to and trusting of. This is the quality of self-motivation whose destiny lies in knowing what it wants without doubt or hesitation. The one quality governs the senses of the head. They could suffer problems through the eyes, hearing, hair loss, sinus problems or teeth. If they are involved in accidents it is usually their extremities that are injured.

Lesson of the One Quality

In the beginning of life there is movement, and the first creation is the seed or the 'one.' In the 'one' there is the strong driving force or impulse for singleness or independence. In the 'one' there is the undercurrent or drive for change or the urge to establish freedom from the influence of others. The first impulse of life is separateness and individuality. In our lives it is vital in the development of the 'one' to lay the foundation for future autonomy by starting something that is our very own, something that eventually will grow to provide perfect freedom from the demands of the system.

The system or mass influence demands conformity and the only way to be part of this system and yet be a free creative contributor is to possess this seed of independence. When we have built something of our very own and it has become an integral part of our mind, nobody can ever take it away from us. This 'thing' that we have built can eventually house the very spirit of our life. It is through this 'one' quality that we have the chance to create this 'seed' and watch it grow and develop to eventually produce the flower or fruit, in the years to come. In truth, the spirit or reason of our being will only reveal itself through our very own creation, as a product of our mind and thought, and our effort through time or cycle. Then in the 'sixth' stage or cycle we begin to see the 'one' beginning to exhibit a power or spirit of its own as it begins to carry us by the very force of itself. Of course that spirit is our spirit working and expressing through the creation or flowering of our effort which began as the seed planted by this force of the 'one' quality.

The 'one' provides the power to start something that is consistent with our natural talent, and also prepares us to follow through with this dream or 'seed' effort no matter what the obstacles. The 'one' does not expect something to just drop out of the sky, as if it should be deserving of something when it has not put forth the effort. Remember, the harvest comes many years after the initial seeds have been sown. The excitement of the 'one' relates to being free to start its own personal venture, free to do things in its own way, free to make its own mistakes and to discover its own potential.

The 'one' brings confidence, positivity and perseverance. The 'one' is not so social but it is profoundly creative and unafraid to stand on its own. It is in this aloneness that the mind of the 'one' finds the incentive to create and to find its own direction. The 'one' is capable of establishing a new beginning in that small but personal endeavor that is entirely its own and that will eventually awaken a sense of its own destiny. If we cannot strike out on our own in some way through an independent act of creation, then the absence of the 'one' in our makeup will register as a frustration or a feeling of suppression. In the negative expression, if the 'one' is unbalanced, it can be stubborn and difficult to be with.

Without this quality of the 'one' we will be relegated to a life of subservience, and bound to others for our survival. All it takes to be a separate and free individual is to start a project of your own, and to remember that the tall and stately oak tree began with a tiny acorn or seed. The feeling of energy, vitality and passion is the result of awakening the spirit of life, through the love of life and our work. As early in life as possible we must establish a direction or seed that is a result of a deep fascination with some interest, otherwise our life can be a wasted effort. Living life on a treadmill for the sake of survival is a denial of all that lies within ourselves. In this state of denial we will live without energy, in the absence of passion, and become subject to the negative forces that work through self-pity. The whole life must be taken up in the expression of the spirit as it evolves through time and the initial seed.

The Individuality of the 'one' stems from the urge to be free from the effects, influences and impositions of all other things and people. To be free to create as we choose, to earn our living as we desire, and to do 'our own thing' with little or no interference from external forces is truly a natural or innate compulsion from within all of us. Every human being feels it and attempts to understand and express it in some way. If the 'one' is suppressed through an unbalanced name the frustration can be severe because it is such a strong force. If we do not discover our individuality through creativity then the frustration that is felt can drive a person into all forms of deceitful and dishonest paths in order to be free from the forces, both good and evil, that demand conformity.

Individuality might be defined as that unique quality that separates us from all other human beings. It is that element that compels us to fight for our rights, to be heard and to be understood.(We must remember that we cannot understand ourselves or be understood by others if we have not put anything into life worthy of understanding.)

Individuality is the spiritual essence of our life that is striving to make itself known through some unique or original accomplishment. All problems stem from a lack of individuality. Every frustration, in our work or in our relationships originates in the undiscovered 'path' or unmanifest individuality. As individuality grows, 'freedom' is experienced; freedom from the invisible and visible forces that affect us on the conscious as well as the unconscious levels of influence. It is probably correct to say that most people react to the pressures of life as if there was something external to themselves that was responsible for taking away their freedom. While there is indeed a very powerful influence working through our society to undermine the 'individual,' the problem is mostly solved through the process of individualization.

If a person is functioning on a creative plane much of the time, they cannot be easily influenced by a corrupt system. If we rally too much to change the 'system' and get caught up in the struggle for change, we may commit the greatest crime of all, and that is robbing the time of the spirit or creative spark. If we wait for governments to give us our freedom we will wait an eternity. Governments can really only produce positive change as the intelligence of the mass consciousness changes through spiritual education. Then 'public servants' will naturally respond and conform to what is truly good for the whole and not easily give in to the pressures of the political lobbyists seeking to advance their personal cause.

Individuality will lead a person through the pressures that demand conformity by virtue of the power of discrimination. By this I mean that our freedom from the powers that demand conformity grows in the light of what is *actually* good for us, as opposed to what we are led to believe is our duty or our responsibility.

We are all a part of a system of 'economics' that is designed to produce food, manufacture goods and in turn create jobs in order to survive. Where does the enormous pressure to survive come from? What is the problem? Is there a shortage of food? Is there a shortage of manufactured goods? Is there really a shortage of work or just a lack of ingenuity to create work? Why does the average person struggle so hard to survive? Was it meant to be that way? Are we to 'bear our cross' stoically believing that life is 'tough' and there is no way out of it? Do we need a new political ideology or a new system?

The economic 'system' has developed to supply the needs of its people and is managed by those who have worked into the top positions of control and leadership. Unfortunately, all are controlled by the forces of competition and self-interest to a large degree.

Since early times, before and after the industrialization of the world, we have all been a part of a huge organized labor force. Without labor or work nothing would be produced. Under the present way of things there would be no food, clothing or shelter if we did not support the system. In times before the `organization' of labor, people produced more for themselves and were perhaps a little more independent or more autonomous. With the industrial revolution everything changed. Without individuality we seem almost forced into labor. Today if we want food and clothing we must work. Very few people's work day is an expression or extension of their noblest ideals and natural talents.

This is not a debate on whether this 'system' is better or worse than any other, but it is a matter of principles and justice. At the present time the 'system' has become complex, competitive and demanding of the laborer's time and energy in order to keep it functioning. It is run by scrupulous and unscrupulous characters whose function is to maintain their positions and their vested interests. It has grown, it seems, with very little consideration of the spiritual needs of the individual.

The true reason and the ideal for the 'system' in the first place should be 'to provide the goods of the earth equitably and justly for the benefit of all' so that we can get on with the real work. The motives for the present 'system' are not for the consideration of the laborer but of course for the sake of productivity and profit. In other words, to sustain the system itself. This in turn has created an unhealthy competitiveness that fosters an attitude of work that is based upon the idea of "each man for himself." Work should feed the soul, not just the belly. It has been said that "to work for self is to work for disappointment."

We have been encouraged by a Protestant work ethic and other questionable ethics that we have a duty to God, Country and the Boss. Not so many years ago we heard that "work never killed anyone." We gathered around our friend's grave and exclaimed with the parting words of grief that " he was a hard worker," as if that was the measure of the person. Today we hear a different cry, to the effect that "work is killing everyone."

It seems that our system of education along with religion has taught us to become responsible to the 'work place' first. For an average of twelve years and five hours a day we are educated and trained to fit into the 'system' with almost no idea of what it is actually going to do for us beyond earning money. At an early age we are led to believe that a good education is going to lead us to happiness. That is an illusion and a lie. Given a choice between instant wealth or the chance to continue your present work, what would you choose? To my amazement, for all the education that is available there is almost nothing taught about life itself, either in the academic or religious institutions.

The 'system' has grown blindly by the force of competition, greed and power. Even the people at the top of the heap have no control over its path of destruction. It will chew you up and spit you out if you try to stop it. It has become a demon without a conscience and without a body.

We have become dependent upon this 'system' for our personal survival. "We must keep business going or we collapse" is the cry. We praise it and worship it as a free market system worthy of world-wide acceptance. We are absolutely controlled by it. We know it produces enormous stress so we create programs to "manage stress." We are on a treadmill from which there is no escape. A rat race.

I have heard it said that "competition may be the life of trade, but it is the death of spirituality." This is so because this system forces the mind to focus exclusively on 'how to survive.' We must remember that any system is only as good as the people that run it. So what is the solution to this problem of economics and its pressures upon the individual?

Almost any 'system' could work if the ideal was right and the people that made up the 'system' had integrity, honesty, trust, compassion and a spirit of good will toward others.

What then has this got to do with 'individuality'? Life is work, but our work should be an extension of our creativity or our individuality. Most people work under a pressure that they do not understand. They are controlled by the forces of the 'system' that demand conformity; a system that has been set up and operated by people without an 'Ideal.' Even they suffer the inequities of their own ignorance and have become powerless to stop the destruction. Because of people's dislike for work they spend millions of dollars on games of chance or lotteries hoping to win the 'jack pot' so that they can end the agony of the work place. We change from job to job, trying in vain to find the right one.

Most of us are attempting to escape the responsibility of work because we have not taken the first step to discovering our individuality. It is our individuality that gives us our power to govern our own time, to work in our own way, to work by our own rules, and to function as a creative force within the bounds of our own principles. It is in fact our principles that give to us our individuality and finally our freedom and our independence.

If we cry out too loudly that the 'system' is unfair and demand that the 'system' give to us our just dues we may unwittingly be surrendering our power to it, and in consequence we may find ourselves dependent upon it.

We gain our freedom by right of our individuality. Even when we are working for someone else, if we are truly individual, circumstances tend to conform to the requirements of the individualized man or woman. Individuality moves away from conformity and towards cooperation. As they say in the east, "When the mass moves in one direction, the Master moves in the other."

Our individuality then, removes us from the pressures of the marketplace. It grows with and because of our talents. It becomes a real thing as we build or put something unique into life. It could be in the area of business, science, art, music, or philosophy etc. The spirit of life actually moves through individuality to provide a sense of confidence, patience or faith in a continuing future that is yet to unfold.

It is fair to say that most people suffer from an uncertainty about their future that forces them to scramble and struggle in an effort to survive. They work from a base of fear and responsibility to feed and clothe themselves and save money for an uncertain future, and even if they secure enough money and goods they cannot feel satisfied.

The problem is a spiritual or philosophical one that is not solved solely through achieving financial independence or planning other economic strategies. Being rich or poor has very little to do with it. Reaching a level of individuality awakens the creative spirit, and the mind then responds to life's responsibilities with an eagerness to make a contribution. The motive then is not fear but inspiration. The mind then may still desire money and other things, but that ceases to be the final objective, and in that case there is no preoccupation with getting and spending and its accompanying fear. You might say that combining your vocation with your avocation is the final solution.

If you have a dream, a vision, or a passion for some purpose, that dream will pull you with it and force you to think and grow, and then your mind and spirit will expand as your vision unfolds. If there is no vision the mind will be held captive by the small things, and the problems around the small things.

Not until a person's path becomes clearly defined will they escape the forces that demand conformity, and emerge as an individual. Each person must find that seed or project that will grow and bloom and eventually release their inherent power or spirit. Our individual growth depends upon it. It is like the emergence of new life within the womb. There is nothing quite so precious to that mother-to-be. So it is to those few who find and commit themselves to something precious that they can call their very own; something that can become a passion for the rest of their lives. Like the mother to her child, the connection is so deep that it could never be abandoned. There is the saying that applies to a rare few in life, "Many are called, but few are chosen," and it is those few who find or create for themselves a true pathway that eventually brings fulfillment and self-discovery. Nothing is so pathetic and sad as seeing people in decline who have not reached a satisfactory completion in their living and their life. So therefore, we must call upon the 'one' if we are ever going to set ourselves on the path of individuality. We will never be free men and women until we do what we want to do as an expression of our deep passions.

When the 'one' is out of balance through the name, or if it becomes too predominant, it robs itself of the capacity to experience life much beyond its own self-interests. Then its major difficulty is in relating to others. It cannot see another's point of view because its basis for measurement is exclusively from its own experiences. As time goes by the 'one' reacts to being misunderstood by withdrawing and favoring its own ideas exclusively. Its judgement of others produces a solitary existence. The older it becomes the more difficult it is to find any pleasure in the company of others, except in a rather casual way, dealing with subjects of discussion that never go very deep. The pity of this one-sidedness is that they can never feel and know that there is more to life than what they can conceive as they react to life from their perspective. In this unbalanced state they become personally attached to their thoughts and ideas, which makes it almost impossible for others to debate with them, and so they lose their objectivity and never experience detachment. In the detached state two minds can agree or disagree with each other's thoughts, and because they are above personality the debate can be stimulating and insightful. In this state a great respect and camaraderie can develop. On the other hand, when the 'one' is unbalanced, debate turns into argument and the debaters close off to each other.

Character and our very spirit evolves or grows as we solve each and every problem related to the growth and success on our pathway of work, and then only if our work is designed to benefit life. It is by the strength and force of our character and our talents that we avoid being part of the herd mentality. The understanding of the 'one' quality marks the beginning and most essential step in the pathway to individual freedom.

Now the 1, 2 and 3 quality relate to the passions and the passions must be understood if there is ever going to be any spiritual progress individually or collectively. We know passion is a great driving or motivating force. Passion can be awakened through a profound interest for something or someone. The subject here relates to the passions between two people of the opposite sex. Male and female represent a duality in that they will always be drawn to each other to satisfy the urge for oneness. We continually seek a connection and a dialogue with those who would relate and respond to our deepest thoughts and dreams. The truth of the matter is that our minds attract accordingly. We generally find in our lives those who are anything but what might be called our soul mates, that is until we understand what a soul actually is. Mind will always, and usually unconsciously, go to where it is according to its level of growth. In other words we usually draw people into our lives that we deserve, and that relate specifically to our inherent weaknesses. Therein lies the test and the opportunity for growth.

All numbers or lessons from one to nine are steps leading to compassion and love in the highest. There is no urge so constant, deep and thought-provoking as love. There is no urge so subtle and potentially obsessive as the compulsion to experience and be satisfied through love. When we *fall* in love we surrender blindly. The power is then aroused through the sexual channel and we are opened to each other and to our own goodness. In this case it is a promise that cannot be sustained. In the highest sense the spiritual force is awakened through sound and the spoken word, or simply through meaningful dialogue. Each lesson from 'one to nine' is leading us to a final union with our own soul and a union with other souls. If we cannot feel, sense and consciously respond to the impressions from within our own soul or purpose in life, it is presumptuous of us to think we could attract a soul mate or mates. Man and woman are here to be help-mates, walking a common path. A spiritual path cannot be assumed. We will never attract a help-mate until we open to who we are, and what we are to offer to life. There is one true reason for a man and a woman in coming together and that is to empower each other through their common purpose. Life's greatest satisfaction is in being understood, but we must first be found worthy. The unique function of men and women is to achieve a self-conscious realization in our conversation with each other. The deeper and wiser the mind is, the more profound will the connection be with another. If two people have reached a high degree of personal awareness and can merge their interests, they can then draw each other out for ever greater self-discovery in their dialogues. It is to a high purpose that two minds should share an attachment, and not to each other's petty needs. If it is the latter, when their personal needs have been satiated their relationship will stagnate A person should always reach for thoughts that take them beyond personality. In familiarity there will always be contempt and fighting will never end.

To further illustrate the meaning of the passions of the 1, 2, and 3 quality it is appropriate to mention the relationship between the nine numbers or qualities, and the ancient study or theory of the Chakras of the spine. Much has been written about the almost mythical power called Kundalini, that like the coiled serpent, lies sleeping until awakened. These awakened centers or 'Chakras' provide the wherewithal to demonstrate certain mental powers, practical and phenomenal.

This knowledge comes out of the East and seems to be attributed to the Indian philosopher Patanjali who lived thousands of years ago. What little is recorded of this man's work leaves the idea that through techniques associated with meditation and exercises in concentration, these Chakras could be activated, and until they are, they remain sealed and their powers dormant.

This ancient record of Patanjali's along with more recent writings of people who claim direct experience with kundalini power leave us trying to imagine just how this power is activated. With a few it just seems to happen spontaneously and nobody seems to know how or why. Meditation may facilitate an experience but is not the basic or leading factor that will open these centers. Using meditation to access the mystical element within the mind is asking for trouble. In most cases where the power is awakened I would wager that it is not sustainable.

A mystical experience can occur because of a trauma that may provide a momentary insight into the mystical realm. Some of these experiences are illusory, some are real but all are momentary.

The reason I bring up this ancient study or theory of the Chakras is because it relates directly to the numbers or qualities from 1 to 9 and will help in the explanation of the growth process or mental development. It is through the gradual development of mind that the Kundalini power rises to energize and activate the Chakras. Each Chakra relates directly to each number quality from 1 to 9.

Exercises in asceticism are of little use unless the mind is focused on purposeful work. We are all here to demonstrate a heaven upon earth through our actions, attitudes and work. Our work should be directed toward the 'greatest good for the greatest number.' Our individuality grows with our projects and the very spirit of life moves in us through our work as it relates to our purpose.

The Chakras or psychic centers represent points of contact for the life current as it travels up the spine. This Kundalini or life current is activated by the breath and is directed up the spine through understanding and living the mental lessons associated with each step or Chakra.

There are nine Chakras. Five of them lie in the region of the spinal column and the remaining four are in the head. The available literature dealing with the Chakras mentions the existence of seven of them, although there is reference to two more, that are nameless, and another three that deal with a highly advanced state of consciousness. This makes twelve in all.

The first six deal with the mind's attempt at self-mastery, ending with opening the sixth seal or center called 'Ajna.'

We begin with the first three that deal with the passions of man and woman. As the power awakens at the base of the spine it travels to the first center called Muladhara and relates to the concept and lesson of the 'one' quality.

This center governs the solids of the body and awakens the procreative urge. It is here that the lesson of the transmutation of the vital force can be learned. When this center is empowered by the breath, the energy is either directed up the spine to feed the brain or it travels down toward the genital area for the purpose of procreation.

Anyone that has used the power of the breath extensively will know the challenge of increased energy as well as an increased sexual urge. If the mind is strong, the power can be utilized for a constructive purpose, otherwise the mind will be plagued by the obsession with sex.

This is the center of physical vitality. It is at this point that the choice is made to either use the vitality for constructive accomplishment or become carried away with the fantasy of sexual pursuits.

It is from this ancient wisdom of the first three Chakras dealing with the passions that some religions have adopted the practice of sexual continence, or the abstaining from sex as a means of conserving the life force. The idea is to direct or focus the energy toward the contemplation, worship and praise of God, in anticipation of some sort of spiritual insight.

The message here is profound. The lesson or the concept that must be attained is difficult and requires discipline and a deep self-inquiry into the true nature of the power available within this first center or 'one' quality.

It is true that the power must be directed, but not so much towards something so ephemeral and distant to the uninitiated as God. It is from this center that a 'sense' of one's purpose or destiny is obtained. It is toward the germ or seed of our purpose that the power is to be directed. If there is no direction in life, the resulting frustration will always find its way downward into sex expression. It is from this center that the great energy registers through a profound physical vitality. An insight can then occur that leads a person into a particular direction that is very finite and tangible. If there is little mental balance or understanding of the other centers then the force of this center will dissipate itself through frustration and sexual indulgence. It is the power of will and commitment that is awakened here when there is a sense of deep purpose.

You will appreciate that all Chakras or psychic centers are related. They do not stand alone. We do not approach each center individually. We do not necessarily begin with the first one and move up the ladder sequentially. Our mental make-up determines where we are and which center or lesson is to be learned. We must all eventually tackle the lessons related to the passions of male and female if we are ever going to experience a lasting happiness.

The first three Chakras dealing with the passions are intimately related but entirely dependent upon the three that follow. The opening of the final three centers in the head area is entirely dependent upon understanding the lesson of 'self' or self mastery as related to the first six centers.

The explanation of the 2nd to 9th chakra will follow with the description of the 2nd to 9th quality of the numbers.

Two

POSITIVE

Peacemaker, Diplomatic, Fluid Speech, Intuitive, Friendly, Quick-Minded, Sensitive, Soft & Refined, Clever, Can Divine Solutions to Problems, Counselors, Idealists, Dreamers

NEGATIVE

Procrastination Dishonest, Lazy, Passive, Too Easy-Going, Can't Say No, Impressionable, Lacking Ambition & Drive, Indecisive, Always Late, Indulgent in Sweet Foods

The 'two' is the exact opposite of the 'one.' While those with the 'one' quality are masculine and positive, those with the 'two' are passive and diplomatic. The 'two' is a feminine force. It is soft, intuitive and impressionable. Being open and sensitive to the feelings and problems of others, they make excellent counselors. They make good listeners and are extremely accommodating. Because of their ability to merge so completely with a person, they naturally make you feel relaxed and open, and can induce you to reveal and say things that you would find hard to say to anyone else. They are friendly and sociable, with a quick mind and a way with words. Their intuition enables them to divine the nature and solution to another's problems with amazing clarity. They are easily affected by discordant environments. They will attempt to avoid conflict at all costs. They are diplomatic and would never take sides. It is their purpose to understand the heart and mind of their fellow man/ woman in order to bring understanding and harmony to life. This is not an individualistic or a positive force. *They* have the ability to surrender their own opinions for the sake of keeping the peace. They lack confidence to strike out on their own, but work well with others. They are drawn to, and feel more comfortable with the opposite sex. Being impressionable they can be influenced against their own better judgement. They are idealistic and adaptable. They are not physical or rugged types, but work best with others where they can use their charm and their fluid speech. They are not easily self-motivated and can be a bit lazy. At times, the fear of creating issues can cause them to avoid speaking the whole truth. Gossip could be their weakness. Their tendency to be frequently late or tardy can earn them the reputation of being a bit unreliable at times. Caring too much what other people think of them, they could become social climbers. They dress to impress. The women are usually very feminine while the men, if the 'two' is unbalanced, can sometimes appear a little effeminate. They are naturally romantic and touched by kindness and soft words. They are neither emotional nor temperamental, and lean toward taking the passive position. In a world of aggression, egotism and self-projection it is well to consider the natural sense of surrender that the 'two' expresses so well. Their inability to say 'no' can make them feel used. Their desire always to please can lead them into social situations that are shallow, and into conversations that lack depth or substance. Lacking in confidence they tend to procrastinate and are slow in making decisions. They are gracious and caring people whose purpose is to blend and mix with others, and to add the social graces so necessary for a relaxed and friendly environment. Their submissive and open personalities draw others to them for comfort and guidance. Not being a highly disciplined quality, they must be careful not to indulge in sweet sugary foods. Their weakness lies in the kidneys and in the bloodstream. In a depleted state they suffer pain in the lower back. Lack of exercise leads to poor circulation, cold hands and feet, as well as swollen ankles. They also suffer through bladder problems, and are susceptible to diabetes.

Lesson of the Two Quality

The next stage of growth in the 'two' is quite the opposite of the 'one' in its influence as a passive force. Now we make progress through our social contacts or through the assistance of others. The 'two' must be understood as the duality of life. In the womb, after the egg is fertilized, it divides itself into two. In the process of life there is a division of the universal cause into the basic life principle of duality. In this duality lies an inherent attraction of opposites or the urge to come back into oneness or unity.

In the 'one' there is only 'self' while in the 'two' there is an openness to receive help. There is a desire for dialogue and friendship. This is to be used for the purpose of furthering your effort and enhancing your life. The excitement of the 'two' relates to opening and merging with another. This stage of development is the time of germination. In the 'one' there was little need of others, and now you should be aware that you cannot do without someone to help you. In life we have all experienced loneliness and the need to share our thoughts and feelings. There are people out there who can help us clarify our thoughts and our direction. The 'two' allows us to be open and to attract those people whom we can help, and those that can help us.

This is a time to experience the pure pleasure of another's company. Time spent in deep and meaningful conversation with another should never be considered as wasted time. In the 'one' we could experience the spark of our own creative ingenuity, while now in the 'two' we can experience the satisfaction of plumbing the depths of another's psyche through good conversation. In the 'one' there was little interest in picking up the phone to engage in conversation for conversation's sake. Now in the 'two' we can more easily feel and respond to the thought of coming together with our friends, and in drawing them out in conversation.

The lesson of constructive association is a most valuable lesson to be learned and carried forward in our life. Because the 'two' is a passive quality it seems that little is being accomplished in our time with others, but in truth we are being nurtured. Our lives can be profoundly enhanced in our business and in our personal lives through living in the 'two.' With the 'two' there is greater ease in our conversational abilities. There is a stronger attraction to the opposite sex. On the negative side there is also a tendency towards gossip and procrastination.

With the 'two' there is a greater need for more rest. It would be wise to understand the value of what we might call an open heart. To truly understand the need and the way to merge with another soul brings lasting happiness. The drawing of one mind toward another must be understood on the deeper level or the results can be disastrous. The 'two' merely brings the necessary openness that contains within itself the power of attraction. The personal advantage to us of this power and its use depends upon our intelligence and our intention.

The beauty of this influence is in being drawn out and in giving someone else the chance to be heard. This is the basis of friendship and a profound source of nourishment for the soul. The secret of longevity is revealed in the merging of souls. The 'two' is only the beginning of the understanding of true dialogue. If we can draw from the 'two' it will teach us how to surrender or open to another mind and soul.

This is an impressionable quality. With this quality you should neither use others selfishly, nor let yourself be used by others. The energy or passion of the 'one' is awakened through our interest and fascination with something of our own. Now in the 'two,' we have the chance to become passionate or energized in our deep relationships with at least a few people. If we cannot meet the criteria that is the essence within the attraction of minds, we will not draw from the energy that is available. If we cannot feel the excitement in our dialogue with others, we will not be vital enough to move to the higher levels of life and living.

Even though it seems a paradox, the urge to 'share' our life or to be with others stands right alongside the urge to be 'independent.' These are two aspects of the same universal life current or spirit. All single qualities must be perfectly balanced or reconciled with each other. If they are not balanced the person becomes inept in some way in dealing with the problems of life. For example, if a person is too independent they find merging with others quite difficult. If they are too submissive, they cannot stand on their own and so on.

Only when we have achieved some level of independence and individuality can we successfully merge or live with others. The 'one' always comes before the 'two.'

We must learn to satisfy and understand the urge that draws us together individually and collectively in our marriages and friendships, and in respect of one nation to the other. This powerful attraction between peoples must be understood from a spiritual perspective, otherwise we will wander around fighting each other forever, looking everywhere for that one person who will finally understand us, or that one nation that will be our ally.

We need to be understood. There is no standing alone. The pleasure we gain from sharing or merging with others is very nurturing. There seems to be a restfulness, a completeness, a natural attraction that stems from fragmented pieces trying to come back together to create the whole. Then why do we say as we struggle with each other, "We're damned when we do and damned when we don't" or "We can't live with and we can't live without each other?" There is a profound lesson here. It seems that the problem of creating and enjoying a good relationship is as difficult as trying to achieve independence. Interestingly enough we find ourselves or our individuality through solving the problem of association, and never through running away from each other. Conversely, we learn to better cooperate and unite with others as we define our own path and establish our independence. I would say there is more potential for human advancement through the lesson of association than through any other field of endeavor.

The passive element within the human psyche allows for openness and acceptance of all other human beings. At this point there must be no discrimination between race, color or creed. Discrimination should only be used to distinguish between truth and fiction, not to alienate people of different backgrounds. We unwittingly bind ourselves to those people or things that we have an aversion to. Dismissing people from our environment may remove them from our presence but it does not remove them from our deep psyche. As it has been said, our hatred as well as our love binds people to us. The dilemma must be resolved through learning to be accepting of others.

When we have learned to be open we can then experience the magic that accompanies acceptance of others. If we are conditioned to discriminate, or are suspicious of others from fear, our heart, and then our eyes reveal it, and close us to friendship. Our eyes must reveal a willingness to invite another into our life. We must submit to them so that they feel that we care enough to listen with interest to what they have to say. The great power of submission is discovered in the midst of a dispute. If the mind is strong enough it consciously withdraws from its fixed position and gives benefit to the other's thought. The one who is conscious of such an action has the control and the power.

When the blending is complete the magic occurs and we are free to speak our minds, to reveal to one another our deep secrets and to open up and say things that we could not say otherwise. We discover a fount of knowledge within ourselves that has been suppressed and then released through yielding and allowing a friendship to develop. Our speech becomes more spontaneous and we are given a chance to explore our ideas because of our connection. It has been said, "When two or more are gathered together in my Name, so am I there also." In other words, there is a spiritual force present when two or more are united in the deepest possible level of communication.

The whole meaning of relationships is to share in the inquiry of life and not to use each other as a soundboard for all our problems. To experience true friendship is a privilege so profound that the feeling is of deep gratitude. It brings the best out of us and makes us feel complete as if someone finally understood us. We gain self-esteem and a confidence in ourselves.

The secret of course is in learning how to maintain and continually develop new friendships. Familiarity and dependence always leads to contempt. I think of a marriage, when the bridegroom carries his bride over the threshold and into the bedroom. There the marriage is supposedly consummated or made perfect as the meaning of the word implies, as if sexual intercourse could grant automatic friendship. If these two people are truly going to be united through love of each other they will have to pass through an initiation process that very few people *understand* or could *withstand* for that matter. In the highest sense the 'consummation' usually occurs well into their marriage, if it occurs at all. What usually happens is that familiarity takes on a permissiveness and a feeling that we have certain rights over our partner.

The 'urge' to be understood, acknowledged or recognized is the basis for the continual conflict in association with each other. It is the problem of egotism. The struggle for understanding and acceptance diminishes as we are recognized for our wisdom and our kindness to others. The feeling of being understood grows with our worthy contributions. If we paint a beautiful picture for example and someone comes along and says how much they appreciate the work, we feel truly understood. If we produce nothing in life we will never have the experience of being understood.

We must be satisfied and happy in our relationships with others before we can advance in our spiritual growth or awareness. We must learn to 'give in' or to submit to others and realize that we do not have to 'give up' anything except perhaps our egotism. The 'female' who is symbolized as the passive or submissive element does this so well while the male is always afraid of being taken advantage of and is less cooperative and yielding. She recognizes her power without great displays of authority. We must all learn to be submissive in the highest sense and to stop fighting each other. For this we need great in-depth experience, first with the 'two' quality, then the 'four' and finally the 'eight.'

When the 'two' is out of balance or too predominant in the name, it creates a shallowness and a verbal spontaneity in conversation that is purely self-oriented and pointless. It loses the strength to stand up for itself and plays it safe by avoiding any meaningful dialogue. When this happens its life becomes small and limited to personality, gossip and those things which revolve around a critical analysis of others.

The second Chakra called Svadhisthana governs the fluid functions of the body and awakens the strong attraction between the opposites, male and female. At this point, we have the opportunity to experience divine communication between souls.

Initially the power of the second center manifests as a feeling of romance between male and female. This power can be moved upward by the mind through an elevated concept, or it moves downward by the force of our negative desires and is then dissipated. The attraction between the sexes is an invitation to discover its mystery. If the mind is not deceived by illusion and has raised its concept to a universal perspective then the 'seal' is removed and there is perfect union through surrender to this person and to our own power.

The challenge here is one of sublimation and purification of mind and desire, as it relates to the attraction between male and female. It is a matter of raising the basic feeling of attraction from a base level to a level where two minds merge in concept. Then there is an automatic surrender into a complete oneness of thought, with its profound affection, which requires no body contact at all. When opposites come together on this level, the principle of duality is satisfied and the result is total relaxation. Only then is communication possible. When this center is sealed, attempts at communication are merely exercises in pretense, and a game between adversaries deciding who is right and who is wrong and who submits and who forgives. In the more immature states of development between the sexes, the attraction and the conversation are dictated by physical needs.

The priest, nun or monk who tries to sidestep the issue of male/female involvement may inadvertently thwart the power moving through the second Chakra. In this case several things may happen. There could be a perversion that takes place as the deep affection, hidden within the sexual impulse is suppressed, or in time the mind submerges the impulse and ends up living in a state of inertia and mediocrity. This of course does not only apply to those who have taken vows of chastity. It is not living a life of chastity that is wrong, but the fear of male/female involvement that can lead the mind astray. Sexual climax, orgasm or ejaculation may be an imperative for the perpetuation of the species but it is not a requirement for spiritual growth. To most of us who see our own mortality and have no fear of our sexuality, then our romantic and sexual experiences can serve to be our greatest teachers but only if we want to see their hidden message. The healing power, in the deep affection between men and women, waits to be discovered by those who come together to serve life.

Three

Positive
Self-Expression, The Power of Emotion, Motivated by Love, Musical, Artistic, Happy, Magnetic Personality, Generous, Philosophical, Ambitious, Imaginative

Negative
Intolerance, Drawn into the Wrong Crowds, Argumentative, Scattered, Impractical, Start Things they Don't Finish, Too Emotional, Untidy, Lacking System & Order, Can't Save Money

The 'three' represents the power of emotion, inspiration and love. It also represents the power of speech or verbal expression. Those born with the major life lesson of 'three' have a magnetic and vibrant personality. Being emotional, they require an artistic and creative outlet, free from monotony and too much routine. It is their purpose to inspire others through their enthusiasm, their love and warmth, and their artistic creations. They make excellent speakers and stage performers. They love music and dancing and have a natural appreciation for color harmony. They are of a happy and playful disposition, full of fun, with a mischievous tendency. They excel as debaters but once drawn into an argument it is almost impossible for them to pull back. They will argue that black is white without knowing why they do it, and strive always to have the last word. They thrive on and are motivated through inspiration. If they lack the more practical and stable aspects of life, they invariably fail to follow through with many of their projects and ambitions. Being an emotional force they are subject to mood swings, but also being of a naturally happy disposition they bounce back quickly. Finding it difficult to finish the things they start, they need encouragement and support in their endeavors, otherwise they can be scattered and undisciplined. They are sensitive and easily hurt. They respond quickly to kindness and affection, and they never hold grudges. They are generally open and loving to all people. Being basically happy, they dislike being in environments where there is sickness or suffering. Rather than responding in sympathy, they would strive to make humorous comments in order to make people laugh. Love being a motivating force in their lives, they must guard against being drawn into love situations merely for sense gratification. They must learn to understand the male/female attraction and to use it wisely. They are generous and giving types and love surprises and surprising others. They can be the life of a party. They dislike hard and monotonous work. They need to be free from boredom, and need to be able to express freely amongst people. Unless they have been disciplined to complete their tasks and to achieve success, they can become lazy and self-indulgent. They are not naturally inclined toward business and materiality but excel where they can express their enthusiasm through music or the performing arts. Their charm makes them good sales people. They are poor in mathematics and technical matters requiring concentration and attention to detail. The 'threes' are optimistic, fortunate and even lucky, but find it quite hard to stabilize their efforts. To the 'three,' money is to be spent for the enjoyment of life, and saving it becomes very difficult. They are showmen and know how to make a good impression. In sports they play for the excitement and the fun, but if a game becomes too serious they lose interest. When disciplined, this influence with its imagination, can express and create on any artistic level. They are closest to their purpose when they can see their influence upon others. They inspire us through speaking, singing or performing in some way. They must be careful not to become indulgent in food and alcohol. Their weakness lies in the liver, gallbladder and the skin. Too much sugar and acid in the diet can result in rashes or other skin eruptions.

Lesson of the Three Quality

In the 'one,' 'two' and 'three' quality we have the 'Trinity' or the principle of thirds wherein all of life is contained. It represents the Father united with the Mother to produce the Child. In the 'one' the seed is planted and then germinates in the 'two,' and finally we see the shoot appear in the 'three.' The quality of the 'three' is the power of emotion and the expression of love. In the 'one' we have the sex urge. In the 'two' we have the attraction of the opposites as a feeling of romance. In the 'three' we have the complete union as experienced through love through the spoken Word. You must understand that love in the highest is expressed through sound as it manifests through the spoken word in the form of wisdom, which ultimately expresses through the lesson of the 'nine.'

The force of the emotion in the 'three' makes it difficult to apply itself to the practical and business aspects of life. No matter how much the 'three' wants things to be organized, the effort seems to scatter itself. The purpose of the 'three' is in the expression of its emotional power through artistic endeavor, and to use its love and charisma to inspire others. With this influence a person will laugh more often and more easily. At times getting the more practical things done can lead this quality into sheer boredom. In the next instant, if the opportunity to escape arises, they can be instantly transformed and energetic. The 'three' possesses the power of persuasion and is easy to be with. As the 'three' puts out love, it is returned with equal force.

The 'three' is a further extension of the social qualities of the 'two,' but uses its influence to inspire and to entertain others. The 'two' is passive while the 'three' is quite active. The speech of the 'three' is empowered by its emotion which enhances its debating skills as well as its tendency to argue. The 'three' has so much enthusiasm and optimism that there is a strong tendency to overinflate its mind with possibilities and expectations that may never be realized. This overly optimistic enthusiasm can swing the 'three' into bouts of depression that are usually short-lived. They bounce back quickly.

It may seem quite irrelevant to many, but to develop this quality through engaging in some artistic pursuit will pay great dividends in the sum total of life's enjoyment. Life is not all work and business. Deep meaningful and loving contacts are vitally important for our overall success and well-being. The expression of our emotions through music and art is crucial if we are to understand the nature of love as a power of influence, and not merely as a thing to indulge in selfishly.

It is through the power of the word, which is the essence of the 'three,' that we make headway in this life. The powerful emotion of love and the power of the word are intricately woven together. Love affairs can take place through the 'three' influence and fail because of a lack of understanding of the true meaning of the word 'love.' The feeling of love is a powerful tool to inspire others on to greater accomplishment. Love in the highest sense awakens through dialogue and is sustained through purpose. The lesson in the 'three' is to learn to love others for their sake and to progress on the basis of using this influence for the benefit of others. The deep personal rewards in life are through giving of ourselves through the spoken word.

I would say that life's first experience with the spiritual essence is in the bloom of our youth when we fall in love. It is really our first contact with the 'spiritual' force of life as it registers through the passions as a feeling of love. We are transformed and lifted beyond the mundane. The impression left is so strong we will do almost anything to recapture it if it is lost. We can become obsessed in the quest to find that one person who will understand us because in the sensation of love we feel understood. The love experience, no matter how brief it may be, can lodge in our psyche and our memory to become the focal point of our very existence. You might say it is the very reason for our existence.

It is interesting that such a profound sensation of love is associated with the physical union of male and female through the sex act, and that the conception and production of a child is accompanied by such a beautiful feeling. If there is sufficient love, intelligence and compatibility in the people engaged in sex, and it is a conscious act with a child in mind, not only is the sexual experience heightened, the result will be passed on to the child.

It is important to note that the coming together of male and female into a condition of complete surrender to each other does not have to produce a physical arousal. Our obsession with sex stimulation has blinded us to the fact that sexual arousal and the feeling or current of love are separate elements. It just so happens that in the sex act they both come together but only if there is some level of genuine appreciation for each other. If we become addicted to the sexual arousal that awakens the love force, then eventually the action of physical union can degenerate to a mere physical sensation and an obsessive need for orgasm with a total absence of love.

With a little bit of reasoning it should be plain to see that taking someone to bed to engage in sex was never meant to be the ultimate way of awakening the love force and sustaining it. We have debased the sexual act as a means of release for our frustrations and a therapeutic promise for a good marriage. How absurd!

Few people it seems experience the love force as it awakens through a mental channel, as male and female come together in total surrender to each other to embrace in a condition of trust, openness and mental inquiry. In this state the union is so complete and the charge of energy so profound that there is complete rest and peace. The result is the opening of a channel of communication and a flow of new ideas wherein two people become as one. In this state there is a profound feeling of love without physical arousal or the need to engage in a physical union. This is because the nurturing element brings such satisfaction that there is no need or desire for anything else.

In the usual contact between male and female so little takes place in their dialogue that the void created usually leads to a desire for sex expression. Most people seem not to be aware that it is possible to open the channel and experience a profound love without having to be aroused physically.

In the physical union there can also be a mental connection, and to some degree the channel of communication will open to allow for the experience of true love, but in this case the union cannot be sustained.

In order to reach the point of opening the channel of love through the mind rather than through the genitals there has to be a sustained level of spiritual perception and not a preoccupation with sexual gratification.

At the heart of most people's sexual arousal there is an undetectable ego crying out to be soothed. The sheer loneliness and lack of being understood drives people to the sexual plane. When the mind becomes more mature and responsible there is a growing awareness of the profound sense of dependence on one another that can be created through sex. The sexual force has the effect of bringing people very close to each other as well as binding them to their mutual weaknesses.

Now they must either commit themselves to the growth process or engage in the continuous fight that inevitably leads to separation. If they are strong and intelligent they will see the opportunity for learning about themselves and the chance for individualization.

The sexual element or the 'serpent' as the Christian message implies "is the most subtle beast of the field." It has its right purpose and its wrong purpose. Some religious theories prescribe total abstinence or sexual continence which can eventually lead to a spiritual awareness if the mind is thoughtful and wise, or it can lead to all forms of sexual perversion if abstaining is premature, or if it becomes an exercise in deliberate suppression.

The passions of man and woman are an intrinsic and essential part of the sexes and not to be dispensed with but to be understood and used constructively by the mind. The lesson contained within the passions is difficult because the pleasure derived is so great and the consequences so profound. If the mind has not reached the point of objective inquiry then the passions literally take over.

If the beauty of the attraction between male and female is construed as a purely sexual impulse then we will never open the door to a spiritual union. If we can look into each other's eyes and respond to the excitement by moving the feeling upward instead of downward, we may discover a beauty that is rare in the experience of humanity.

If the mind is ever going to be a fit instrument for the spirit, it has to be free from the effects of a desire nature that is governed by sense-dependence. There have been many books written on the subject of the sexual energy, and how this can be used to experience higher mental states when arousal is channeled by the mind, and orgasm is withheld. This can be accomplished, but only when the mind is strong enough to bring the emotional state working through the nervous system to a point of rest. Normally, the arousal produces an excitement that agitates the nervous system to such a degree that control becomes impossible. The result of prolonged agitation is depletion of the vital force in the bloodstream.

As the mind becomes more sensitized and creative, these exercises become unnecessary. They are usually exercises in avoiding the real work, and they could become an excuse for the weak mind to further its sexual fantasies. The degree of the depletion of the vital force, or the awakening of the spiritual force, is entirely dependent upon the level of the evolution of the couples involved and their compatibility. It has always been known that creativity and sensitivity to higher thought impressions require a conservation of the vital force. Today it is still not accepted by the medical community that there is usually a depletion of the vital force in the bloodstream through sex. It may be true that most people are not aware of any depletion, but when we are trying to draw from our sensitivity in order to enter into the creative process, the depletion becomes very apparent. If we are going to be thinkers, vital force and energy are of the essence.

It should be said that as the mind moves away from sense stimulation which includes sexual stimulation, it enters into a previously unknown world. This does not mean that one is not capable of or open to sex and other areas of emotional response. It is just that now we can begin to experience a clarity of thought beyond the incentive of the emotions. The motive force in our life is no longer a constant and unconscious desire for things to feed the emotions. Now there is a certain freedom to explore the unknown world that is made available through a natural sensitivity that has opened the mind to a level of greater creativity and to a more selfless existence. This is a place where the ego cannot enter with its infinite number of petty and selfish demands, pulling us into every kind of inconsequential problem that is its way of perpetuating itself. A good parallel is of a rocket ship fighting to break through the force of gravity and into outer space where the rocket is now free to roam the outer reaches of space without any external pressures or attractions. This illustrates the possibility of the mind moving beyond the desire nature and its obsession to be fed. This represents the eternal struggle as humanity strives to bring the dual forces of life into a state of equilibrium.

I should conclude by saying that the passions should never be feared but should be experienced with an inquiring mind in order to locate their proper place in the scheme of things. We should keep in mind that when there is no discipline over our passions, we will tend to seek out an endless number of theories designed to perpetuate and satisfy a sexually indulgent nature.

The number 3, the 6 and the 9 relate to love and are progressive steps revealing the ultimate pathway from self-expression to the expression of wisdom as the spiritual teacher. In the 3 the love force is awakened and is experienced more as an emotional and sexual sensation that needs to be understood and expressed constructively. In the 6, the power moves into responsibility. At this point and in the midst of physical arousal and love-making, a strong thought emerges for the creation of a child. This actually enhances the love-making and deepens the connection and the giving to each other. In all three numbers the urge for communication is awakened and progressively advanced. Finally in the 9, the love force is moved from passion to compassion and awakens the teacher within the individual. Those with 'nines' in their make-up seldom bring forth the highest and the best out of themselves, but drop to the level where they become preoccupied with sex because that is the only way they have been able to momentarily glimpse the beauty of love.

We all desire the love of someone of the opposite sex. A love that promises closeness, support, affection and the restfulness of being understood. This is obviously the attainment. The mind attracts others according to where it is in its level of growth. The great lesson of the 'three' relates to tolerance. We will draw many different types of people into our lives. Some of them will be compatible, some not, but all must be understood. In many cases, even our children or our parents will be quite distant to ourselves in thought, and yet we must learn to live with almost anyone, and in the process learn to tolerate and be tolerated by those who are different from ourselves. Eventually, when the lessons are learned, we find that our own expression and thoughts are welcomed with greater interest, and we gain the respect that allows us to be more complete or full within ourselves. If there is a soul mate or mates that would bring greater completeness to each other, then it would seem that it is something earned when we satisfy the criteria for spiritual attainment. The realization of the promise and the dream of loving and being loved would then bring the physical (emotional), the mental and the spiritual aspects of relationships into a single complete whole.

The 'three' in the unbalanced state, or when it is too predominant, becomes too intolerant of others and cuts itself off from deep connections. Its argumentative nature, rather than inspiring others alienates them. They then seek out love relations through the sexual channel and can never be satisfied. Their speech is both an asset and their greatest liability. Those with a predominance of this quality in their name find that their efforts are scattered and incomplete through a lack of follow-through and self-discipline.

In the highest, the gift of the 'three' is in its power to debate points of view. Through its quickness of thought, through debate, its perceptions grow very quickly. Through verbal exchange it expands upon its own ideas and spontaneously finds new words and ways of explaining its thoughts. Debate becomes the stimulant of the mind. It challenges and is challenged for the sake of truth. Anyone who has evolved their debating skills, to a high degree, can awaken a spiritual force that can be felt by all. This is done when the intention is to serve and enlighten others. In this case the power that is awakened draws the participants together in warmth and camaraderie. If there is sufficient intelligence within the group consciousness, the energy drawn forth and released into the atmosphere can be mystical and leave people in awe and in silence.

The third psychic center or Chakra which is called 'Manipura' represents the culmination of the first two and awakens the power of love. This Chakra governs the emotions of a man and a woman. If the mind has become strong through concept and is no longer prey to the intoxication and deception of the passions, it can call upon the spiritual force of love as it expresses through the *spoken word.* At this point emotion can be transformed into inspiration.

If we truly understand the basis of the attraction between the sexes, and work to develop a deep appreciation and understanding of each other, then two souls can experience the profound sensation of union or of finally being understood. This level of understanding brings with it a profound sense of relaxation.

If the mind can traverse the subtle barrier between the impulse for sex and the element that lies behind that impulse, the seal is removed from the third Chakra and 'speech' is awakened. If this is accomplished a profound sharing of thought occurs. Here it is that the mystery of spirit as it moves along a current of sound and the spoken word is revealed. It is at this point that the exquisiteness of debate is experienced, not for the sake of proving someone wrong but to actually stimulate the mind and deepen the connection with your opponent. The analytical process that accompanies constructive debate is an essential experience in self-inquiry. The power in and behind the spoken word emerges as the debate closes in on the essential truths of any subject.

FOUR

POSITIVE	**NEGATIVE**
Practicality, Reliable, Patient, Persevering, Logical, Scientific, Deals Easily with Facts & Details, Methodical & Efficient, Analytical, Intellectual, Orderly & Mathematical	Discontent, Fussy, Skeptical, Small-Minded, Lost in Details, Too Physical & Instinctive, Too Materialistic, Lacks Depth, Mentally Slow

The four is a mental and intellectual force expressing through logic and fact. It is the purpose of the 'four' to inquire into the reality of life, through form and practicality. They have the endurance and patience to pursue an idea or project with concentration, and they can focus on an infinite number of details. They are methodical and thorough as researchers. Being slow and precise, they resent being pushed. Their inclination is towards science, mathematics and the more technical aspects of life such as mechanics, computers or anything requiring attention to detail. Not being of an emotional nature they conserve energy and have a great capacity for hard work. They are strong with great physical endurance. Their strength is also in their ability to go forward step by step and to finish the things they start. They are not idealistic or inspirational. They follow and pursue only those things which appeal to logic and reason and only those things which fall within the limits of the five senses. Once their minds are made up about anything they are extremely slow to change their views. They can be skeptical and even stubborn. They can become lost in detail and quite fussy about inconsequential things.

Everything about them is orderly, and they must live to a specific routine. They are neither spontaneous nor impulsive in their actions and movements. By comparison to the other qualities the 'four' appears to be a bit drab. They are not particularly interested in music or the arts. It is to the 'fours' that we owe all of our technical and scientific advancement. When balanced, it is a keen intellectual force missing nothing and always demanding proof of any particular point of view. This is not a driving or ambitious quality, but it is stable and persevering. They lack confidence but will work diligently in order to make slow but steady progress. 'Fours' are very studious but they restrict themselves to those subjects which are classified as non-fiction. They love to putter around the home and feel quite secure with a family and a few friends. There is little desire for travel or change. They are workers in the mind as well as having a capacity to create with their hands. They can work with equal precision in such fields as carpentry, engineering or accounting. When unbalanced their lives can become very narrow, mediocre and lacking in vision. They are ingenious when working with problems dealing with mathematics or complicated aspects of any type of research. Their patience is almost unbelievable when they are required to research a project, and time is never a limitation. They lack imagination and a depth of feeling for things. In matters of love they lack romance and tend to be a little too physical. They have an appetite for heavy starchy foods. The 'four' governs the stomach and intestines. Constipation is their main problem. Blockages in the intestinal tract can lead to such things as colitis, growths or cancer in that area.

Lesson of the Four Quality

In relating the 'four' to plant life we observe growth taking place underneath the surface where a root system is being developed, and the growth above ground seems to be momentarily halted. So it is with our effort, there are times when there is nothing we can do to move a project forward. We are forced to work patiently without too much expectation. The reason why there are so few people capable of success through mental growth is because of a lack of follow-through, perseverance and patience. To make anything work requires an in-depth concentration, constant correction and a tremendous analytical ability. These qualities are aspects of the 'four' and relate to the ground-work or development of this root system.

Truly successful people would concur that patience is indeed a most prized possession and one that is most difficult to acquire. If we cannot learn to endure the pain and disappointments of our everyday life, success will not be ours. Pain and disappointment are and must serve to be the stimulant for thought. The 'four' represents the awakening power of intellect and logic. If the mind cannot sustain a certain clarity in the midst of difficulties, then it can never understand and experience the enormous power and inspiration in solving its own problems. Patience allows the mind to concentrate and focus the thoughts without giving in to defeat. Again and again the mind is forced to be patient when things break down and plans seem to fail. In the 'four' all the energy is focused on the details of the object, and for the moment the larger vision or picture of life is obscured.

With the development of the 'four' quality we can see the weakness of a thing and seek out ways of improvement. We must all endure the pangs that are felt when things do not turn out as expected. Only those who have learned the lesson contained in the 'four' can understand the infinite power of thought. While the rest of the world is seeking an escape from a problem the 'four' is using patience and the power of intellect to bring forth answers. The 'four' is unwilling to abandon the endeavor and will concentrate upon the problem until the solution comes. This represents the stuff of success.

Change seldom produces growth except when it arises out of a natural process that is a continuation of a past success. No matter how much we rant and rave and suffer the pangs of self-pity, life will not reveal its mysteries until we realize that all things are conceived through mind, thought, analysis and repose.

We presently live in a fatalistic society that believes we cannot solve some of our own problems, and so we turn them over to God and common religion. It is through the 'four' that the mind learns of the virtually unused power of analysis and concentration. In the 'four' we learn the value of 'marking time' or waiting patiently, even if it takes many years to reach the answers to our questions. The conviction that there is an answer and that it can be found will leave the mind open to the ultimate solution in time. Being patient in the meantime is the beautiful quality of the 'four.' Life cannot be all dreaming and desiring. In the 'four' we enjoy becoming totally absorbed in our work. This is a time to study the effects that difficulties have on our emotions, and to learn to endure them for the length of time it takes to see into the problem clearly.

Learning to THINK ultimately brings the gift of insight and perception. This is the reason that every evolving human must pass through the tests of life and time, over and over again, and do so with a minimum of complaint. Patience could be described as the power to sustain a mental focus until the mind brings the desired result. *It is not a mental condition of long suffering.* If the mind cannot sustain the position of concentration and confidence toward a positive outcome, then it will lapse into emotionalism and self-pity. It is pathetic to see the physical and mental distortions reflected in the bodies and minds of aging people who have spent their lives escaping from their problems. We must learn to face our imperfections and use the power of the 'four' to weave a thought pattern that brings forth answers. There is tremendous strength to be gained and carried with us into the future if we can learn the lesson of the 'four.' It is wise to learn that all good things come out of the stillness or patience of a mind that has learned the art of contemplation. It is not altogether the final result of our efforts that should sustain us, but also in the capacity to live happily in the moment, knowing full well the time will come when we shall experience a reward commensurate with our thought and effort.

When the name carries too much of this quality of the 'four' the mind gets lost and preoccupied in incidentals. The conversation of those with too much 'four' revolves around material concerns. Then their lives become limited to an interest in things related to the five senses and they fail to see the larger picture of life. Their fussiness can drive people away. Their conversations can border on the mundane where they become rather dull and uninteresting.

The 'four,' 'five' and 'six' qualities are the lessons relating to the development of the mind and intellect. The four opens up a fascination with fact and form and loves the intrigue and question of what makes a thing work. We are presently in the middle of a 'four' great age or 729 year cycle that has ushered us into a time that is governed by scientific thought, mathematics and industrialization. The smaller cycle within the larger one, from 1944 to the year 2025, is an 'eighty-one' year cycle that is also a 'four.' What is obvious about the 'four' is that it is capable of in-depth research and study, and contributes to life from the position of science and fact but only as it relates to form, technicality and mathematics, or the outward manifestation of life and movement. In consideration of the idea that all things work or evolve in balance or relativity to each other, science will never, by itself, solve the more pressing questions of man's and woman's humanity to each other. This deeper question must be resolved through a more philosophical analysis and research which relates to the higher numbers.

The fourth Chakra is called 'Anahat.' Ana means infinite. Hat means boundary. This lesson relates to consciousness. If we think of the terms unconscious, conscious and super-conscious we may get a better grasp of different mental states and the lesson of the 'Anahat.' Mind in the unconscious level is still being moved about by the forces of emotion, desire and impulse. In other words, it is still being influenced against its will and higher reason. In the conscious state the mind is able to apply reason and thought through concentration, and begins to understand the relationship between the forces of cause and effect, or problems and the reason for them. In the super-conscious state the mind links itself to the divine essence or reason of its life and now lives for that purpose. In the 'four' or fourth Chakra the yogis, as the literature relates, draw upon this Chakra or force, through a concentrated effort to demonstrate the power of levitation. The theory is that this center governed by 'sound' and the force of concentration, can be drawn from to perform astounding mental feats. Whether levitation is a truth or a myth, it is an interesting idea. We should keep in mind that an even greater feat or at least a prior one, would be to use the mind and the power of reason to achieve daily happiness.

FIVE

POSITIVE	**NEGATIVE**
New Growth, Ambitious, Reformer, Versatile, Quick Thinker, Lives for Freedom, Promotional, Loves a Challenge, Fearless, Independent, Self-Motivated, Creative, Stands for Truth & Justice	Too Restless, Quick-Tempered, Moody, Self-Destructive, Indulgent, Unstable, Verbally Cruel, Chaotic, Too Intense, Unsociable, Candid, Vindictive, Driven, Never Finds Peace of Mind

This quality represents action and change. Its purpose is to seek truth and justice in all things. It is for the 'five' to challenge the old order for the sake of new life. Those with this quality are reactive and dynamic reformers. This is a highly creative quality demanding freedom at all times. It is an intense mental and intellectual force capable of great achievement. They are creative, versatile and can accomplish much in a technical or artistic field. Their drive and motivation are aroused through a challenge, and once the challenge is satisfied they have a tendency to lose interest. If unbalanced, their lives could become a series of uncompleted projects. Their curiosity and seeking natures compel them into an infinite number of pathways. Their search for answers is never-ending. This quality in particular requires a knowledge of life and a purpose, otherwise their intense nature will be reflected as frustration and self-destruction. When challenged with a project they are ingenious in quickly working out solutions. Their minds are quick and clever. They are afraid of nothing, and when backed against a wall they will come out fighting. They can be cutting and sarcastic in their retaliation against an injustice directed at themselves. Their restless natures need to be satisfied either through travel, sports or other types of adventure. They are like "a rolling stone that gathers no moss." They are independent, serious and generally lack humor. This is a quality that learns through experiences, and often bitter ones, and usually at a cost to themselves and others. They can be skeptical with strong likes and dislikes. They follow their hunches and can sometimes be subject to premonitions. Their lives are the most crucified, because their fundamental purpose is to challenge, and depending on the intensity of their challenge, it is returned with equal force. They must guard against becoming vindictive. They must learn to move through their anger in order to discover a truth, and when they do, they can literally move mountains. If they cannot control their moods they will revert to self-indulgent activities that can destroy them. Their intensity can make them impossible to live with. They never forget a slight, and when their sense of justice is abused they often have the urge to get even. They can be impulsive and live to regret some of their actions. They are very trusting and will take you at your word, but their naivete is sometimes their downfall. Their daredevil attitude and their gambling instincts make them quite fortunate in games of chance. They are formidable competitors in sports or in business. They make excellent sales people and promoters. In an unbalanced state they are extremely impatient and find it almost impossible to create relaxation and peace of mind. Their intensity and restlessness can interfere with their ability to fully complete their projects, and hence they move on before they grasp the full worth of any endeavor. Sleep is almost impossible for them when they are either excited or worried about something. The 'five' governs the solar plexus, and because of its close proximity to the stomach, they are prone to stomach upsets. These people can suffer nausea and stomach ulcers. If they do not have a purpose that provides a challenge they can be subject to extreme depression or moods.

Lesson of the Five Quality

The 'five' represents rapid growth or the branching out of our efforts and accomplishments. The 'five' provides the courage and the incentive to move out and try new things. In the highest sense it represents the search for truth. Life will provide the experiences through the 'five' necessary to awaken us to a greater sense of ourselves. It forces us to move through the pretense in our relationship with others. The five is the quality of the activist, striving for social change and justice.

The four, five, and six are elements of the mind and the intellect that must go through a purification process. At this point the intellect is forced to develop and gain the position of knowing through analysis based upon principles and truth. In the 'five' the mind scrutinizes everything in search of truth, or that thread that will allow for progress, change and freedom. It is inherent within the growth process to challenge and to be challenged. The reason for this is to establish greater clarity of direction and meaning to our endeavor. If you are indeed growing through the 'five' you will come to a point in your endeavors where you will be confronted with opposition.

It appears that in this stage of growth there are forces that are trying to stop you in your efforts. It is through the 'five' that we must fight the good fight and discover what the truth is in our endeavor. In other words, do we really believe in what we are doing, and do we have the courage to keep on? No one that has experienced success, and changed life for the better has been able to avoid the challenges from the forces that demand conformity, and these forces will do anything to prevent change. This has to be faced. The battle must be fought and won, over and over again.

In this lesson is the stuff that produces strength of character. It is at this point that a person discovers the power in truth. If once the mind can comprehend, in the midst of the battle, the element of truth, then the battle cannot be lost. This truth is like an awakening certainty or realization that provides an indomitable will. Here a distinction must be made between the force of anger that can be the drive behind an effort, and the motive power that is there when a truth is discovered. In the former, the forces that are aroused cannot be overcome. In the latter the way will be found to produce change, or change will naturally unfold with positive consequences to show us that truth will prevail in the end. Our anger towards an injustice may be aroused initially. Then we must we look closely at the reason for our fight and discover a truth within ourselves and usually about ourselves. If we do, we should find to our amazement, that the anger dissolves, and a new way is found that subdues our critics, and leaves us to do our work.

Freedom and independence are the trademarks of the 'five.' The impulsive quality present in this influence can move you into many and varied experiences with the purpose of finding just that right thing that is best suited to carry you forward in your effort. As the 'five' stands at the end of their life they are usually amazed how much more they have experienced by comparison with others. There is no mental or spiritual progress made until the mind comes into a strong personal conviction about its purpose and the truth of its own ideas. If you are not challenged from the outside, you will never be challenged from within yourself to discover who you are and what you can do for life. Like the 'four,' the 'five' is here to awaken the mind to thought and analysis, but it is applied in a different direction. Those individuals who come into the 'five' or develop this quality are driven by a force for change and new life that cannot be stopped. It is this driving force that is necessary for any growth or advancement of the individual. This motive force awakens through personal resolve, or a conviction so strong that nothing short of death could prevent its forward movement. When the established or ruling forces attempt to interfere with any positive and sincere effort of an individual to promote new ideas for the benefit of life, that individual enters into the possibility of arousing the dormant force of the 'five,' which lies at the very core of the search for meaning and truth.

Societies and whole cultures contain elements both progressive and repressive. They can work to benefit the individual and to suppress them. This also applies to virtually all institutions and organizations. If we lack the power of the 'five' we generally play it safe and go along with the status quo. Simply being part of the mainstream force is not sufficient for those on a path towards spiritual progress. If we wait for the prevailing forces to evolve and to carry us forward with them, time will catch us short of our goal. The five is such a dynamic force and contains within itself an intuitive response to a truth or a falsehood, particularly when it is blocked in its endeavors. It just knows when it is facing the lie, and when it will have to confront that lie if it wants to be free of its influence. These untruths are a part of all of us through our cultural and religious conditioning. We must all reach the point when we are forced to confront the stagnation which is prevalent within our institutions and their unchangeable dogmas. The forces that are behind the established institutions are powerful and do not want change. They are here to preserve their interests and their positions. They are embodied and disembodied. We all contain the elements that hold back the progress and evolution of life. These obstacles are integral parts of our religious and secular perceptions. They must be challenged and dealt with as we perceive them within ourselves. To root them out takes a courageous soul.

When you discover that the elements within your intimate connection with things dear to you are actually holding you back, you will come face to face with your phantoms. Therein lies a fear that seems too strong for the average person to deal with. We should keep in mind that the struggle and challenge is not so much the need to change society as it is a struggle with oneself. It is a moving away from those things that represent stagnation and death. The reason it is so difficult is because it usually requires a severing of our attachment to things and to people. In our intimacy with these things and with people comes the fear of loss, criticism and alienation. The solution is simply a matter of right perception. If a person can draw from the power of the 'five' they will find the strength and the will to change, and then take the consequences that will follow. The positive result is a greater sense of freedom. As we individually stand free and teach others what we have discovered, these old forces that stand in the way of true progress will slowly fade away from lack of support.

There are those people, usually strong in the 'fives,' that will be compelled to tackle the mainstream force head on. They need our support. The blindness within personal greed and power is very destructive and infects our whole society. The 'five' is here to fight that, but must carefully study its own intentions, otherwise it can become as destructive as the force that it chooses to fight.

Just following along blindly in life destroys initiative and leads to inertia and the death of the mind. Analysis and thought are activated in the midst of a challenge. All great minds derive their motivation from the urge to improve the human condition. The mass of humanity fights for constant change but resists truth. We must remember that change seldom constitutes progress unless it evolves out of completion or an awareness of some truth.

Truth is synonymous with integrity, justice, consistency and human kindness. Growth of mind and character can take place in any field of endeavor as long as it is consistent with truth in every aspect. Truth does not require defending, it can stand on its own. This is an important point. We do not necessarily need to fight against evil or corruption. We merely have to discover a truth in the situation.

If our anger is aroused to the point of it becoming the motive force, the truth will be obscured. We may be aroused into action initially by a reaction to an injustice, but if the reaction awakens the urge to get even, or to defend ourselves, we will surely lose the battle. Evil contains within itself the seeds leading to its own destruction. We merely have to be alert and perceptive to the lesson or truth that the situation holds for us. What we must remember is that the intent, intensity or force that we direct towards someone will be returned to us in equal measure. So it is that "as we judge, so shall we be judged."

If the mind has learned to endure the process and to hold on in the midst of the battle, eventually there will be an insight into the problem and a profound awareness of an obvious truth. If the mind gives in to its own emotion, the battle will go on indefinitely and anger will perpetuate the confusion. We see this every day in the 'soap opera' drama of real life. Our egos keep us in a perpetual fight with one another over the controversy of who is right and who is wrong.

Truth is a rather peculiar element of the mind in that it cannot so easily be taught, or passed on to another, but we can observe it in the few who are examples of nobility and strength. As our mind grows in the light of truth, we are moved in our experiences into ever-changing circumstances, gradually moving towards a greater freedom of individual expression. The embodied and disembodied force that demands conformity begins to lose its power over us as our minds perceive the greater truth. Truth is beginning to set us free. We find that our working environment is changing, our relationships are changing and the power of truth is carrying us with a sense of confidence, and fear is losing its hold on us.

We should all be freedom fighters, and reformers battling the inequities, injustices and corruption in our society. Although, if we have not awakened the mind to the perception of truth we will unwittingly pervert the whole meaning of it, and find ourselves in a continuing battle for power of the most insidious kind. We see this being acted out in senseless wars, between countries, between religions, in politics and marriages. When we finally see what is really happening we will be terribly ashamed that our fighting has gone on for so long individually and collectively.

There is a revelation that comes in the struggle between good and evil. The prize is won by those with the courage and patience to withstand the urge to strike out and injure others. A compassion emerges that is the final revelation.

Spiritual progress demands truth. It has nothing to do with what religion or spiritual practice you may follow. It has to do with perception and insight. When the mind moves into the lesson of the 'five' and is confronted with its own limitations through societal conditioning, the intensity that is awakened must produce change or the 'five' influence within the individual will self-destruct. The 'five' is a very intellectual and independent force when balanced properly through the name. Without the 'five' we will not sustain the effort to move forward. When confronting our own frustrations there must be the courage to experience and experiment in order to break through the fears that tie us to old ways and habits.

I think of how we are tied to our intimates for example, through the limitations that are set through laws and rules set down by church and state. These laws and rules establish our conduct with one another and have the tendency to keep us in our place of stagnation and unhappiness. We can unwittingly destroy each other through boredom and lack of truthful and meaningful dialogue, and fail to realize how important it is to move beyond the limitations of the idea of exclusivity in relationships. We limit ourselves in moving out in our relationships through fear of violating some great spiritual truth set down by our religions, or in the fear that perhaps our weakness in governing our sexual appetites will carry us into prohibited sexual encounters. These may be valid considerations for the weak and the indulgent, but they stand as barriers to the spiritual aspirant. If we start from a place of integrity and responsibility, being fully aware of our own needs, the 'five' will call us into action and into experience. Too much concern and fear of what others may think of us is the greatest deterrent for advancement in life. This is not a debate on whether marriage, for instance, is right or wrong, or whether we should divorce our spouses because they do not give us what we want. It is a matter of how to arrive at a more universal perspective in regards to the need for a more mental or spiritual intimacy with all people in our life. I only use this as an example to illustrate the challenges that must be met by all of us.

Inherent within our upbringing there are a multitude of perceptions that need to be challenged and rooted out if we only have the courage to do so. If we can draw from the 'five' we will not wait for our religious and political leaders to show us the way, instead we will find the way for ourselves. The 'four,' 'five' and 'six' remember, are the lessons related to intellectual development. Mind contains within itself the solutions relating to its own dilemma. All that is required is the power to think. Let no one convince you that you cannot do it by yourself and that you cannot awaken the powers in and behind thought. If you cannot find the joy of creative thought you will gradually succumb to the forces of fatalism.

The growth or unfoldment of individuality is entirely dependent upon the mind's ability to perceive truth. While truth is a difficult thing to define there can be no growth or advancement in life if the mind cannot discriminate between what is right or wrong. Although it is subject to individual perception, truth is nonetheless the basis of progress and is applicable to all things in life. All people are subjected to and governed by the same truth. The 'new age' movement has given rise to the idea of "your truth, my truth," as if each person operated by different principles or truths. This seems to be an excuse for people to justify and seek tolerance or acceptance for their way of life whether it be truthful or otherwise.

We could say that all of our perceptions of life are merely theoretical. This may be so, but if there is to be any progress in any field of endeavor it can only be on the basis of a truth, known or not known. We may desire to send a rocket ship to the moon on the basis of our theories of propulsion, gravity and motion, but if they are incorrect, the rocket ship is doomed to the reaches of outer space, if it even gets off the ground. We may choose to be a homosexual and believe that it was not our choice, but if it is contrary to truth or law it will become an obstacle to spiritual progress. The laws of life are infallible and cannot be bent to justify our particular orientations. We may be plagued with sickness or disease and believe that it is decreed by God, bad luck or bad genes, but ultimately we are responsible. Ignorance is no excuse.

A person may spend a lifetime studying a particular psychology and write books on the subject, but if the basic premise is incorrect their mind will not move forward one jot. Truth is illusive and makes its appearance only when we are on the *right* track. The perception of a truth is dependent on absolute honesty, devoid of personal bias of any kind. Few people, it seems, can be so honest. Any amount of selfishness in the mind will influence our thoughts and cause them to veer towards self-defense, self-preservation and the criticism of others. Where there is egotism there can be no truth. To be so honest requires self-scrutiny, consideration of others and a highly developed intellect.

I have often been involved in discussion with people who become defensive by saying, "I don't have to explain myself because I just know in my heart that it is so." Wouldn't it be lovely if everything we desired and sincerely wanted to believe actually became true. This type of thinking leads to self-righteousness and a mind closed to new ideas. Without the urge to seek truth, conversations become dull and meaningless exercises, where everyone tries to be nice in order to avoid exposure to their own ignorance. It seems we will do anything to avoid the intimacy that truth can bring, for fear of being misunderstood or labeled an antagonist. Inquiry into life and truth brings vibrancy and excitement into conversations, and if the intent is right, warmth and love also.

In ancient Indian literature the 'five' or fifth Chakra, like the 'three,' relates to sound and speech. The lesson is of purification and control of thought and the hasty or impulsive urge to speak with the intent of hurting. In the third Chakra the urge to speak awakens, in the fourth logic is applied and now in the fifth the mind has a chance to separate truth from fiction. Those with 'fives' in their makeup know intuitively and instinctively when someone speaks a lie or is simply misguided in the expression of their thoughts. The power of the fifth Chakra is in knowing you are right in challenging others and putting them straight. You do this not because you wish to offend, but you reach a point where you cannot allow an untruth to be unchallenged no matter who speaks it. At this point you are not afraid of the consequences. You will even invite the criticism of others. When this center is active the mind is quickened and cannot let the lie pass, but at the same time it knows the appropriate response to fit the person and the situation.

The negative expression of the 'five' relates to the uncontrollable impulse to express its opposition of others and of others' ideas and thoughts. The 'five' cannot take criticism and tends to react in self-defense and in time can becomes an outcast due to the rebellion that has been building up through the rationale that "the world is against me."

Six

Positive

Responsibility, Self-Confident, Independent, Paternal/Maternal Instinct, Reliable, Instructive, Intellectual, Serious & Responsible, Modest, Can Accumulate, Knows Right from Wrong, Inspirational & Practical, Can Work for Themselves

Negative

Worry, Interfering, Bossy, Lacks Concentration, Know-It-All, Avoids Responsibility because of Excessive Worry

The 'six' quality represents the mind itself. It prides itself in 'knowing.' It is very studious and knowledgeable about everything and never wants to be found not knowing. Even children, when asked about anything can be heard to say "I know." These people are very mental and intellectual. With this quality we are awakened to our responsibility to others. Those with 'six' as their major life lesson are the instructors and teachers of the race. They like nothing better than to be asked about something. They are very objective in their helping and love to give advice. They are at their best when they are in positions of authority, in fact they are not happy unless they can gravitate to positions of leadership where they are helping others. Their strong maternal or paternal instincts make them the best mothers and fathers. These are very stable people whose lives revolve around home and family. This is a very community-minded influence, with a great desire to take charge. They must never be subordinate to others. They have a versatility like the 'five' without its restlessness and can work with their hands but prefer mental work. This is a serious quality that is always thinking but finds it difficult to distinguish between creative thought and worry. This is the quality that must learn to have confidence in what we might call its inner consciousness, otherwise its worrying nature could present mental problems. Because of its genuine concern for others, the 'six' represents the first step or stage beyond the 'self' and is capable of true individuality and self-confidence. Without balance the 'sixes' will "cross their bridges before they come to them," and assume that there is a problem when it doesn't actually exist. Being the number of the mind, the 'six' blends quite well with all other numbers or qualities. They pride themselves in being self-taught and self-made men and women. Their leaning could be towards the arts, sciences or as entrepreneurs, depending on the other qualities in their names. Sometimes they can be viewed as know-it-alls because they do not rely on others for advice. They are extremely dependable and responsible and can be relied upon to carry out their tasks without help, in fact they resent interference of any kind. They naturally accept more responsibility and eventually rise to positions of authority and leadership. When unbalanced they can be interfering and pushy in their know-it-all attitude, and as parents they can then become bossy and intolerant. Being so aware of the difference between right and wrong they must learn to let their children grow in their own light. They are very confident and understanding in their dealings with others. They need to be their own boss, and in their own business, where they can gain the respect of others for their knowledge and expertise. No matter what their problems are they will always seek out their own solutions. Being the number of the mind, they are generally quite healthy. Their only problem lies in their excessive worry.

Lesson of the Six Quality

The 'six' is the final stage of unfoldment in the middle 'third' of the nine qualities. This is the stage of true self-confidence. Not something that is assumed but that which awakens through the beginning of a true self-realization. At this point the mind's intellectual capacity moves into a more objective analysis because it now becomes aware of its responsibility to others. From this point of view the 'six' is more capable of moving past a personal bias that favors oneself or 'self' (ego).

With the 'six' there is a settling of the mind and a desire for sharing life's experiences. There is a strong 'nesting urge.' In the six cycle it is the best time to physically conceive and the ideal time to mentally conceive of the idea that it takes more than one to create a full life. In reference to the love power of the three, six and nine, the six now applies responsibility and moves the power to the mind where love, separate from the physical plane can be sustained as a force to help others.

If we apply the 'six' to the growth cycle it is the time when the 'bud' appears as the promise of things to come. If the effort has been carried successfully from the 'one' through to the 'six' there should be a growing awareness that the effort is strong enough to sustain itself. This seed or project planted in the 'one' cycle is now in the budding stage and is self-motivating. The mind at this point begins to withdraw from worry and concern, but that is only if the life effort has been a worthwhile one, in service to life in some way. The mind should see that it is alright or acceptable to stand back and begin to rest a little and view its creation, and to have the confidence in perception that its creation has a life of its own.

In all things there is an essence or spirit which begins to reveal itself in the 'six' cycle. It is at this time that we can begin to feel a confidence in the inner consciousness. In religious terms it could be related to faith but in this case it is not 'blind,' it has been earned. Even so, it is the beginning of the 'letting go' process. That is, the letting go of any doubt that the effort could fail. If there has not been a continual and progressive movement, beginning with the 'one,' then in the 'six' there can be excessive worry. At some point in life there must be a surrender into the very spirit of life, and it is at the sixth stage that this begins to occur. The mind opens up to the existence of a cause or reason for its life and effort. This is the significance of the Christian statement, "Many are called, but few are chosen." In other words, many are on a quest but few are chosen by life or the spirit of life to perform an actual function that benefits life and others. When this path is found there is no denying it. One is absolutely committed. It is not a matter of choice. The spirit or reason of life moves through you to express a fragment of that which it is. There is no denying or giving up in one's effort, because you are being moved by the very force of your reason for being, and it is in harmony with life.

It is well to consider that the spirit of life or of the individual, awakens through a developed character as it moves through time and cycle, and then only if the mind creates something worthwhile. It then serves as the vehicle for the release and expression of the spirit.

The 'six' is a quality that relates to home, family and stabilization as it reaches out to others to teach and to instruct them in the ways of life. This is a powerful mental influence that gives a person a strong sense of right and wrong, and the feeling that we are indeed our 'brother's keeper.' The 'six' being the quality of mind itself brings tremendous focus and concentration in study and debate. The 'six' understands the meaning in the statement, that to "work for self is to work for disappointment." The development of this quality is the preparation stage for the entry into the higher states of mind of the 'seven,' 'eight' and 'nine.'

Up until the end of the 'six' the effort in life is still primarily an effort to establish our own individuality and our own identity through our own creation. Up to this point our work has been an effort directed for the benefit of using the 'self' as a vehicle in preparation for the 'seven.' This brings the possibility of withdrawing into a deep place of tranquility, and reflection on deeper things, or a further 'letting go.'

The 'six' represents the total individualization of the mind and a complete mastery of thought forms. The mind at this stage is no longer subjugated by "the Genii that rule the earth." Now there is an understanding of the true meaning of self-confidence. There is no more worry. Where the money is going to come from to pay the bills, and how to satisfy all the material and body needs is no longer an issue to the mind. The mind now sees that mental tension, being self-induced, is the root cause of all physical and mental contagion and degeneration, and can now begin to see itself moving past these negative influences.

The negative condition or expression of the 'six' through an imbalance or when it cannot achieve self-mastery, is worry. Worry is a confusion in the mind that relates to fear of failure. Doubting oneself relates to lack of confidence in the very spirit of one's life. It is the mind's failure to recognize its link with the natural rhythm of things. The driving force with so many is the fear that they will not survive without tremendous effort and work. Unconsciously, we think we need to worry in order to make things work, and in so doing we merely perpetuate the fear and worry. The gift of life and all its beauty should be our only mental preoccupation.

The 'six' represents the seat of our individuality. It is the number of balance and has the potential to include all numbers or lessons into its life experience. When this happens the mind's perceptions clears away the illusion and the worry, and it realizes how easy it is to survive. Even the most wretched of humans can find ways to survive with little effort, particularly in our present-day societies in the developed world. So why do we worry? It is simply wrong perception. Worry is a negative mental force that influences the mind when the mind's future is uncertain. This negative force is a creation of one's own mind that grows through lack of confidence in an unknowable or unseen future. There is no one that knows absolutely the way their life is going to unfold and what exactly is going to happen from day to day. To the confident mind the unknowable provides a certain excitement. Even the possibility of failure promises change and a lesson learned and a further awakening of the mind to the unseen forces of life. We learn about these things as we understand life's natural rhythms. To those who are more closely tuned to these rhythms, the message is simply to enjoy life in all its beauty and under all circumstances. When in tune to these rhythms, we are able to work longer and more creatively.

At the 'sixth' stage or level of spiritual individuality we learn to relax and to let life come to us. To 'let go' or surrender into this state is impossible to most if they are not motivated by a strong sense of purpose. That purpose begins to form through the lesson of the 'one' and evolves into a greater completion in the 'six.' There is simply no room for worry. It is counter-productive. Worry is a product of one's ego which grows when the life is without purpose. Individuality is a freedom of mind when that mind links itself to reason and purpose. It is well illustrated in the life of a bird who sings in the morning of the joy of living and of the day, never giving thought to whether it will survive the day or not. It responds to its purpose instinctively and it carries out that purpose joyfully without concern, and at the end of the day it sings again. As we become more conscious of our purpose, and the power in being happy, we can awaken the will to simply ignore the tendency to worry. There is a point in which the mind must trust in the past effort to produce a result and then to withdraw and wait. There must be continued work but there is less concern for results. If the work is good and useful, the mind begins to feel a driving force and a greater excitement. There should be a greater response from life at this point. When the fear motive for our life has been replaced with purpose, the mind begins to open to a much greater level of creativity.

There has been much talk about the power of mind or thought, as if our mind could create anything it so desires. This is an illusion giving false hope to people as they pursue their dreams endlessly. In fact, there is probably less than a two percent success rate in those that pursue their dreams. Even if they do succeed at bringing many of their desires to fruition, it is not likely that they will be much happier. I do not say this to discourage those who would work to achieve greater levels of personal excellence in their goals. It is true that much can be accomplished to bring forth one's natural or innate talents, particularly if the right or proper effort is put forth. However, there is only power or passion in the effort if it serves others or life in some way.

If we do not know the aim of life, our achievements will ultimately bring disappointment. Life is like a maze as we try to understand the mystery of it. It is the function of every human being to unravel this mystery as it is woven into the fabric of our personalities and character. There is a blueprint behind every person's life and this blueprint is the very spirit or reason for that life. To go against that blueprint is to waste the energy and the time of the spirit. Those few who commit their time to understanding themselves, know that everything eventually fails that does not relate to purpose. In failure, if they are wise, they discover a little more of themselves. This is not to say that because it fails that "it was not meant to be."

For the spiritual aspirant, the mind begins to discover that it cannot materialize anything that it so wishes. The mind must thoroughly study its desire nature to separate itself from the obsession of attachment or selfishness. The higher one climbs into the mental realms the greater the chance of failure if the mind is not directed with the proper intent. The power of the individual mind grows by degrees as it conforms to the blueprint, which after all is simply the right perception of things.

The power of the mind is not in its ability to acquire things, but in its capacity to understand the meaning or reason for its acquisitions. We can drive ourselves crazy for the want of things and succeed only in suppressing the spirit or life force within ourselves. The power behind thought is released only when the thought is properly motivated. We cannot simply entertain a thought and hope it will eventually become a reality, but we can certainly achieve happiness daily if we come to understand all that lies behind our desire nature.

Therein lies the success in the practice of self-inquiry or in self-realization. The bulb or seed of the daffodil will not produce a tulip. It is therefore a waste of time to pray, to yearn for, to rant and rave, meditate or to think positively on those things that are foreign to our true path. How to acquire those things that are essentials should be the object of fascination and concern for the mind. To acquire sufficient wealth to survive is not difficult, but to prevent an obsession with the effort takes wisdom. It happens every day that a man takes to himself a good woman, but few of these men develop the wisdom to overcome their intolerance of her imperfections. The obsession with our problems obscures the vision of our pathway. The knowledge and wisdom of the progress of lessons through numbers is the key to mental evolution.

All is mind and thought. It is appropriate to consider how the mind operates and brings things into form or materialization. Things become manifest in our lives according to the predominant number qualities of our names and birthdate. If the nature of our thoughts and desires are relative to these qualities, then it is very likely that we will achieve our ambitions. If not, all the desiring, praying, ranting or raving will be in vain. The results of our thoughts and desires are consistent with the rules or laws operating through the mind and life itself.

Desiring, praying or wishing for things does not guarantee the materialization of the desired object. Prayer is an entreaty or an asking for something from someone and then wondering endlessly if your prayer will ever be granted. This leads to fatalism and the perpetual question of whether you will ever get what you want. It is better to ask the question of yourself, "How will I get what I want?" We may pray to our gods for peace, but if we cannot conceive of how wars begin through greed, hate and possessiveness, and weed those things out of our minds, we will wait an eternity for our prayers to be answered. It is easy to ask, pray or desire things, but to be worthy of receiving anything, our thoughts must meet all the requirements set down in the book of life. God the reason, becomes involved in all form, visible and invisible and evolves according to its own rules pertaining to each individual form. If we humans break the rules of right living and thinking, through ignorance of them, we must suffer the consequences. Everything happens according to the nature of our thoughts.

To make things happen then, requires the development of our true or innate talents. Our talents enlarge our field of opportunity. If the mind learns to think early enough, it will not slip into the concepts of fatalism, wherein it loses its confidence and its self-reliance. It is so easy to conjure up our images of gods and idols as objects of worship and sacrifice in order to get what we want. We must understand that it is in the nature and operation of our thoughts that anything occurs. If we cannot learn to originate new thoughts and ideas on our own, we will never experience an increase in our level of happiness. If the negative forces of our mind that express themselves through our suffering and self-pity cannot be challenged and dissolved, then our minds will remain a prey to our endless and unrealized prayers and dreams. If the object of our desires or prayers is unrealized, the mind can become obsessed with the craving or yearning for that thing. The desire for money for instance can become a distraction and a preoccupation ultimately destroying the mind's ability to be happy. It should be the pursuit of the meaning to your life that takes up your time and interest, and then let the acquisition of things fall into their rightful place.

Prayer can become a denial of the very spirit of our existence. This spirit emerges when the mind is inspired through the pursuit and discovery of truth. It is not necessary to ask anyone or God for anything. It is better to ask *yourself* a question which then prompts the mind into thought and action. To do otherwise is to deny your own divine nature. All that is necessary is to thoughtfully follow your questions to their ultimate solution. It is the weakness and deficiencies of our mind that represents the problem. We are not denied earth's bounty and the exquisiteness of living because of our lack of prayers, but because of our lack of understanding of the nature of our mind and thoughts. There is great vitality and inspiration when the mind and senses are disciplined to allow for creative thought. It is the function of religious and academic forms of education, to serve the individual in understanding how the mind develops, and not to get lost in the worship of personalities and other useless pursuits.

It is understandable why people give up so easily and revert to a passive resignation to a host of gods and professionals to solve their personal problems. Our thinking must first be based on a thorough understanding of the theory and principles of life. These will serve as a reference point as we pursue an idea, otherwise the mind can easily go off at a tangent. The spirit or power of life is accessible to those who mentally awaken, by degrees, to self-realization through thought. We must be careful not to put our minds to sleep waiting in expectation for the answers to our prayers, or to be gullible to the host of theories that promise enlightenment as a diversion or escape from the responsibility of serious thinking. So it is the qualities or lessons of the 4, the 5 and finally the 6 that awaken the mind and intellect to an awareness of its own spiritual nature.

Here at the 'sixth' step we are at the very threshold of true life and living. The 'six' has been symbolized as a child in white, representing purity. In the Christian writings it is stated that, "Except that you become as a little child, you shall in no wise enter into the kingdom of heaven." Heaven of course is a state of mind. The symbol of the child has been used to suggest the absence of worry and the pure joy of living. The senses of the little child are open to the exquisite beauty of life, even as the adult should be, but seldom is. In the 'six,' the promise is the mastery of worry. In the 'one,' we begin the individualization process by creating something that is entirely our own. This first step separates us from the influence of the masses. We should have taken that project started in the 'one' to a final conclusion in the 'six.' Self-mastery or spiritual individuality is the sixth step. In other words, if the projects begun in the 'one' have become our life's work, the mind begins to let go of worry and experiences a supreme self-confidence. There can be no doubt about success. We are now working for life in the absence of self-serving motives. This allows the mind to give up worry altogether. Worry implies an egotism or a preoccupation with one's petty fears.

At this point, the ego is beginning to die. True individuality implies a sensing of one's purpose or a knowing about life, sufficient to allow for a flow of increased energy, along with spiritual insight or the spontaneity of original thought. In the absence of worry, the mind and senses are naturally open to the beauty that life has to offer. The child has it naturally because its senses have not yet been covered over with wrong perceptions. As children, if our minds were to continue their natural unfoldment through true spiritual education, can you imagine where we could be today? As adults we must undo so much of what we were taught.

Those who draw from the highest aspects of the 'six' can awaken the paternal or maternal element within themselves. They can create beautiful families and homes where the atmosphere is nurturing and full of joy. It is no mystery to them, why some children go bad. Creating beautiful children out of love for them is natural for those who can access the wisdom inherent in the lesson of the 'six.' Creating a deep link with your children is one of life's greatest pleasures and sources of nourishment.

The sixth Chakra called 'Ajna' is the first of four centers in the head and relates to individuality. It is written in the Eastern wisdom that Ajna is "the seat of consciousness" and when this Chakra is awakened the mind comes into "conscious thought and discrimination." It relates to the lessons dealing with the control of the passions. Only when the passions are correctly understood can the mind be free and able to function creatively without constantly being drawn into sexual awareness. In other words, the relationship between male and female is brought to the highest possible level. The potential love that we expect from each other should bring the mind to a more restful position in order to free itself to consider things outside of its emotional and physical needs. In a true union between spiritually compatible males and females, the nature of the love connection is more affection and warmth, and consequently there is less of a need for sexual arousal. In the quality of the 'three,' the feeling of love is awakened and difficult to understand beyond the excitement of body attraction. In the 'six,' the feeling of responsibility is added to the attraction and the physical arousal, along with a profound desire to produce a child and share in its upbringing. Those who have the 'six' in their makeup will feel the sexual arousal heightened by the thought of producing a child. In the 'nine,' the love force opens up to an even greater perception of love, as it moves the mind toward a more universal and less personal perception of our relationship to each other as male and female.

So it is all dependent upon the development, in the 'six,' of one's intellectual capacities. Therein lies the power of will to eventually become a master over our moods and negative thought impressions. Worry is eliminated by a simple exercise of the will, but only when a person is ready to dedicate one's life entirely to the greater purpose. Then greater purpose becomes the central focus and not the worry. At this point, God the reason or the life force is felt as the supportive and carrying influence when we consciously choose to be happy. Through the power in the breath and a concentrated thought we can move our mind beyond any mental disturbance.

It is in the mass or collective mind that most transmittable diseases originate, first as vibration and then as sickness. The individualization of mind frees itself from that influence. Self-mastery through learning the lesson of 'six' is essential if the lesson of the 'seven' is to be learned and experienced on the highest level.

SEVEN

POSITIVE

Philosophical, Deep Thinkers, Sensitive, Refined, Quiet, Love Nature, Intuitive, Theoretical, Moved by the Mysterious, Studious, Reflective, Intense Concentration, Ascetic, Stoical

NEGATIVE

Inner Turmoil, Too Introspective, Moody, Lack Verbal Expression, Repressed and Jealous, Dreary, Overly Sensitive, Lonely, Secretive, Affected by Noise & Crowds, Live in their Senses

The 'seven' awakens a deep sensitivity to the mysteries of life, nature and the invisible forces that operate behind and beyond form itself. It is the purpose of those with the 'seven' to use their sensitivity and their intellect to translate these forces into religious or philosophical theory. They feel things more deeply than others and are drawn to nature with its animals and all of its beauty, and quickly become absorbed into its tranquillity. Being so sensitive, they seek to protect themselves from the crass commercial world, by surrounding themselves with the refinements of art and literature, and to place themselves in an environment of peace and quiet. They are reflective and studious with great powers of concentration. They can become deep and philosophical, particularly if they develop their natural ability in writing. Life always forces them into positions of aloneness, and contemplation of the deeper things, because of complications in communication with others.

This is the most misunderstood quality of all. They tend to lack an easy and fluid speech, and will avoid being put into a position where they have to express their ideas or points of view verbally. They literally close down from nervousness or apprehension if they are made the focus of attention. If they are not overly sensitive, they can be drawn out in conversation on the deeper aspects of life, but they are not good in small talk. They can create an awkward silence that will force you to speak first. If they become offended in any way their silence can create an icy chill. On the one hand their sensitivity can allow them to draw from profound levels of creativity and thought, but when disturbed they have a most difficult time in controlling thought forms and their feelings. Their greatest difficulty is in controlling their moods and in passing unfair judgement upon others. They must learn to forgive others and to be open, giving and loving toward people, otherwise they tend to become reclusive and unsociable. People seldom live up to the expectations of the 'seven.'

Their natural sense of mysticism draws them into the realms of religion and philosophy, but they can also be drawn into the occult with its fantasy and imagination, dealing with matters that could never be proven. They enjoy the sensation of mysticism that comes with exploring the unknown. They must learn to apply logic to their inquiries, and to seek inward for the deeper truths and the reason for life. In occupations, they thrive best out in nature, or as artists and writers. They have a deep appreciation for music and reading, and are quite soft and romantic types, reveling in moon rises, sunsets and quiet walks along the lake shore.

When unbalanced, they can be quite shy, and uncommunicative. They can be gabby in order to cover up their own sensitivity and to avoid revealing their true thoughts. They will not allow others to become too personal with them. They must learn not to live too much in their feelings and their imagination, but should strive to develop a keen intellect, for they have an enormous potential in mental creativity. Their weakness lies in the heart, lungs and bronchial organs. They can be asthmatic, and only they know what it is like to take a deep breath without feeling satisfied.

Lesson of the Seven Quality

In the 'seven' the mind is compelled to consider that which is beyond form and materiality. If it doesn't, life can be quite difficult. In plant life this is the blossom time or a promise of the fruit. We have now actually entered into the final 'third' or spiritual qualities represented by the 'seven,' 'eight' and 'nine.' If the mind is to unite with spirit or the reason of one's life, there must be absolute tranquility through the moving away from the profane, the crass, the pretentious and the superficial aspects of life. The spirit of life will not reveal its secrets through the mind until it becomes insightful and devoid of useless things and thoughts. This cannot be done through meditation alone. It is achieved through the gradual process of recognizing the need to create an environment or atmosphere that is outwardly quiet and pleasant, wherein there is a possibility for creativity and refinement. In this state there is no room for indulgence and laziness.

If our lives and time are spent in a preoccupation with material pursuits, there will be an inexplicable inner restlessness that can never be quenched until we come into the 'seven. Those with the 'seven' in their makeup, who have not yet probed deeply and successfully into themselves, will suffer from the misunderstandings and inner turmoil that result from this deep sensitivity. This is because they respond to the imperfection in others as well as within themselves, and fail to interpret the reasons for their discomfort. These misunderstandings should lead the mind into itself and into a deep search for the ultimate meaning to life. The negative and moody expression of the 'seven' produces an unfair judgement of others, in order to satisfy its hurt feelings. The depth of the 'seven' is hard to understand. It represents the first step or opening into the higher realms of thought and feeling. It is beyond the planes of personality and is a great source of peace in its love of nature and the mystery of the transcendent states. It seems that few people dare to enter fully into this kind of depth for fear of losing touch with their friends. They must be careful not to move too deeply into the realms of fantasy and the occult, which drags them into a world of mysticism wherein they find comfort in unreality and in the presumption of spirituality.

I mentioned in the earlier part of this discussion that the highest expression of spirit manifested through sound and the spoken word, taking form as wisdom. In the 'seven,' the first step into the spiritual domain, we are compelled to look deeply into ourselves and our relationship with others to find a true meaning there, or we will be deeply at odds with others and ourselves. It reminds me of a story about a young pupil of a great teacher who asked of him if there was not a faster way of gaining wisdom. The teacher answered that there was, and that the secret lay right beneath his nose. Of course the mouth lies beneath our nose, and the true meaning contained in the 'Power of the Word' is in controlling our speech or moving away from discussion that is pointless, or merely an exercise in hearing oneself talk.

Therein lies the promise of accelerated growth. In the 'seven' there is a sensitivity that runs so deep that small talk and meaningless jabber registers as noise and confusion. The lesson here is difficult because we all crave association, but without depth of mind and depth of connection with other minds it is impossible to draw from our own spiritual nature. What is required is a positioning of our mind in a state that refuses to be a part of pointless discussion and senseless things. The difficulty here is that when we choose to do that, we find that there are few people left in our life. In this self-induced exile from those who would drag us into small-mindedness, the mind must become thoughtful and philosophical, and maintain its position without judgement of others and without withdrawing too far into an introspective state. In this deeper state, the mind is compelled to create or it can go mad with loneliness and self-pity, and then become reclusive and critical of others and of life. When the mind reaches a non-judgmental state and learns the lesson of detachment, the mind moves beyond personality and leaves others be. In this state, we know who we are and how to maintain our position as an individual without giving in to the pressure of the crowd mentality as it attempts to pull us into itself. At this level, the mind enters more easily and freely into a truly meditative state and draws from a source of much greater creativity or receptivity of thought vibration. You begin to perceive that people generally talk too much about too little. This is merely an unconscious attempt to avoid deep intimate mental contact.

Maintaining silence in order to plumb the depths of your own psyche or someone else's, is very disturbing to most, and prompts the uninitiated into meaningless chatter that only serves to break the sometimes awkward but essential silence. In the 'seven' we must enter into the silence in order to interpret the wisdom that can only come out of the silence. Wisdom can only speak or emerge out of the silence of true individuality. You cannot tune into others' thoughts wisely, without absolute mastery of the silence and the focus that is necessary to engage in meaningful dialogue. If the mind is not developed in the balance of all the qualities, it will seek to escape from this silence.

It is well to consider that only the human creature is endowed with the tools of language, speech and distinctive vocal cords that allow for the potential in communicating, releasing and experiencing the divine essence. Human consciousness, being at the pinnacle of life, holds the potential to reveal the very meaning of life. The secret to life is inherent in the *word.* All the great Holy Books of the world make reference to a *master key* defined as the *word.* In other words, our communication or our conversations with each other holds the potential of releasing the *power* of the *word.* It is something to think about.

In reference to the independent states of the one, five and seven, the seven now reaches even higher into the state of separateness or independence where personality drops away as a useless appendage of the ego. As the ego begins to dissolve into the nothingness from which it was created, the senses begin to open and respond to thought impressions from deep within. Even the innocent child's senses are open to the pure enjoyment of life, and so the potential is there in the mature adult to recapture the childlike wonder and beauty of living, but only if they can transcend the ego states and enter through concept, into the states of happiness. There is transcendence first and then meditation. It is raising our mind beyond the problematic state that opens it to the planes where it becomes free and meditative or receptive to clear, spontaneous and original thought.

Poor is the individual who cannot feel the urge for peace and tranquillity in the midst of the struggle; who cannot sense the all-pervasive 'spirit' as they walk through the woods or along the shore of a lake or ocean, or watch the sun go down over the horizon. Are there people who are dead to the feeling of mysticism, as the full moon rises over the mountain peak, or when their gaze is directed toward the stars at night? Have you ever smelled the fragrance of a particular flower or heard the song of a bird, and been overwhelmed by the experience so that the mind never forgets, and the tears rise involuntarily in gratitude for life? Have you ever encountered animals and been unafraid, and held their gaze and communed with them as a brother, or sister?

Anyone who has not awakened the 'mystical' element can never really wonder about the meaning of life and be thrilled at its mystery. *They* can never pursue a truly religious or a complete life. Who has read the Holy books of the earth and has not at least sensed the wisdom and the promise that they hold? Have you ever had a mystical experience that set you on a path of inquiry? Have you ever sat at a party and listened to the noise, the meaningless chatter and the idle gossip, and wondered what you were doing there? There are some of us, who by the very force of our deep feelings for life, are compelled to travel on what might be called an inward journey.

The very force of a person's mystical nature will tend to turn them inward for the happiness that they cannot find outwardly. It should drive them away from the crass, the vulgar and the unrefined elements of our mass, crazy culture. Eventually, this mystic element should awaken the creative spark, the intuitive faculty and a thinking capacity for originality in writing, painting, music, sculpture and a spiritual insight into the greater meaning to life.

It does not require that we join a religion, seek out a reclusive life, enter a monastery or move away from cities to avoid contact with others. We do not have to become ascetics or live to the extremes of self-denial. The mystic element of the 'seven' requires a channel through action and creativity. There is a danger in indulging in the mystic sensation and being drawn into wild imaginings and illogical fantasies dealing with psychic phenomena and weird unprovable theories. These things capture the imagination but lead us nowhere, and have the subtle effect of bloating our egos into believing that we are becoming spiritual, when in fact we are just avoiding the realities of life.

At this advanced stage, we are no longer dealing with the aspects of the material world but with the invisible forces of a more phenomenal order. To attune the mind to this higher level of thought requires a substantially clearer and more sensitive mental disposition without ever losing control through over-sensitivity. To enter into this state requires a very discriminating lifestyle. There has to be a refining process of both body and mind.

The mind at this point must have risen above moods, anger, judgement and all the trivia that preoccupy the lives of so many. The mind must recognize the difference between sense or emotional stimulation, and a higher order of thought and sensation. The mind must have reached a certain degree of self-mastery over the desire for indulgence in the emotional aspects of life that are so pleasurable. All religions throughout time have touched on this idea. If the mind is going to access levels of mental creativity and spiritual insight, there must be a moving away from sense-dependent habits and activities. It should be obvious that great creative people are very disciplined. If there is an addiction to music, food, sex or any other pleasure, the mind is diverted and becomes preoccupied and roams around in a nether world of imagination, desire and obsession. There has always been that choice between the dictates of creativity and the urge to be merely entertained. It is not because we desire to become religiously pious that we choose to be refined, but because it is a prerequisite to the 'open door' and to creativity. Happiness, in fact, is a simple matter of exercising the choice of how we can feel at any moment. Unhappiness, depression or confusion represent a mind out of control.

Turning inward is a process of turning away from useless activities and pointless conversations. In a deeper sense, it is moving away from fear, worry and doubt about the future. It is all about developing a faith or confidence in our inner consciousness. When fear is our motivation, we work to secure our future through pension plans, insurance policies, our children or any other device that promises to look after us in our latter years. This approach serves only to keep us on a treadmill. It is well illustrated with the Christian admonition that you cannot "serve two masters," it is either "God or mammon." The one keeps you confused while the other reveals the mystery of the additional scriptural gem, "Seek first the kingdom of heaven within, and all these things shall be added unto you." It is all about sacrifice, not the sacrifice of lambs, virgins, or any other life forms but of our own lower natures.

These quotes were put down in writing by someone that obviously knew the process. This process can never be achieved through the passive act of becoming religious or affirming your religious convictions. Having confidence is gaining the ability to see the 'law,' in operation. The individual must first be well established on a path or objective, serving some useful purpose in life.

Then as we see the purpose unfolding we also passively surrender to the process without worry. Each step of the way requires letting go of some old habit or way of looking at life, until we gain the confidence to hold onto something we might call 'spirit,' which is without form or substance. We may consider our responsibilities to feed and clothe ourselves and pay our bills but we will have reached a point where worry is seen as being completely counter-productive. It is the conquering of worry at the sixth level that will allow entrance through the spiritual door of the 'seven.'

As the inner path is pursued we enter more deeply into the silence. This silence has nothing to do with meditative techniques. Meditation may induce relaxation but it can never produce the silence, although entering into the silence will naturally make the mind more meditative and peaceful. While offering a temporary relaxation, meditation will never solve the problems of the individual. Entering into the silence forces the mind to think. Going inward does not require moving into the quiet of the forest. Turning inward is simply a figure of speech. Silence is a matter of being very thoughtful. When a person has reached some level of silence they become aware of people's motivations and reactions in the course of conversation. The tendency for the majority is to babble on and on without any significant or intelligent reason. The exchange becomes a dialogue of self-expression or self-interest and always an avoidance of the silence. Speech should arise out of the silence and out of interest for others. Few, it seems, can enter into this silence because it requires great emotional control and an intent of speaking that which is in response to the silence and not to the emotions. When the mind becomes so discriminating, a process of alienation occurs and the inner path is entered upon. We can no longer engage in life or conversation without being conscious of a reason for so doing. If the individual can enter into this path without expectations from others, and endure the loneliness without criticism, then eventually one discovers the true signs of one's own spiritual individuality.

We spend the time of our life in two ways, either with people or by ourselves. When we are alone and secure in our individuality, our senses will respond more easily to the beauty around us because our mind is uncluttered. In this state, the mind begins to feel or sense impressions from a higher source. It could register as an expanded awareness and appreciation of life and nature, or as an insight into some particular problem that we have been thinking about. When we are individualized, our relationship to people will change radically. There will be no abuse of each other. We will enjoy the company of others because of the opportunity to explore life together. The potential for being nurtured through a soul connection with others is enormous.

It is well to mention the danger of imbalance related to this lesson. It has been written that the elements of egotism can take a more subtle form in those who enter into the pathways of spirituality. When we withdraw from the crassness of the masses, it should be because of a natural process and not because of a developing self-righteousness. In the latter case, the mind will unwittingly alienate itself from others and lose the connection with others, which will ultimately lead to great loneliness. While we must see the error in the ways of others, we must also consider the admonition regarding the fine line between righteousness and self-righteousness. In self-righteousness we lose the pleasure and the power in the spontaneity of conversation. Judgment of others closes the door to communication and to humility. This is the trap and the challenge of those who would be spiritual teachers or leaders who are put on pedestals by their followers. If we lose our capacity to connect with all types of people on all levels of development, our minds can become depraved through loneliness. Spiritual hierarchies and cults develop through idolatry or the raising up of others as objects of worship and deification. We will never develop as subordinates, nor will true leaders flourish, as their brother's keepers, if their souls cannot connect with other souls through an openness of heart.

The 'one,' 'five' and 'seven' are the progressive steps leading to independence and individuality, which leads ultimately to the universal state of the 'nine.' In the 'seven,' the mind draws a pleasure in one's own company and in one's own thoughts. If mastery over worry has been achieved in the 'six,' then in the 'seven' there is an even greater confidence that holding to your life's purpose is the *only* thing that matters.

There is imagination, depth and creativity that allows the mind of the 'seven' to conceive and write the most profound thoughts, if it is evolved or balanced. In the balanced state, the 'seven,' being the first stage into the spiritual realm, can be brought to such depths of peace that the senses can open to a more transcendent state. Here the mind is so complete that at times the experience of awe is so expansive that it cannot be shared through speech. In these moments the feeling of gratitude for life and living is so deep that the tear ducts will spontaneously open allowing the tears to flow. At times one is left immobile as if in a trance, where no one dare approach. At other times all the other aspects, numbers or qualities of one's life will expand and be recognized, as power is brought to them. I can only presume that these are experiences that represent the opening of the seventh Chakra. which has been called Sahasrar.

We live in a sea of thought and sensation. We cannot go beyond either thought or sensation. With the knowledge of numbers and their qualities, we understand the process or evolution of mind as it evolves though the Chakras or differing mental states. It is in the seventh center that the mind can experience the highest sensation, that for periods of time is devoid of all thought. This spontaneous mental state of non-thought can then give way to a profound stream of thought that is both original and insightful. Do not be misled by the ideas that there is a realm beyond thought that is the desired goal in life. If you are not careful you can actually put your mind to sleep through different exercises, but mostly through lack of use. What we must achieve is the overall concept of life that will gradually allow the mind to transcend disturbing thoughts, but not thoughts in themselves. The proponents of the 'non-thought' theories can never go beyond their own thoughts. We will experience a spontaneous and continual stream of thought as long as we have language. Only if we remove language and name from the human species will we succeed at removing thought from our life. Then of course we will have reverted back to the animal or instinctive state. Mind is the channel for consciousness. It is thought that eventually leads the mind to higher and deeper levels of sensation. In the opening of the seventh Chakra the mind awakens to life as experienced through sensation or feeling, and to an elevated concept.

EIGHT

POSITIVE

Leadership, Organizational, Even-Tempered, Can Delegate Responsibility, Appreciates Material Values, Ambitious, Desires own Business, Good with Figures, Stable, Has Objectivity, Feels Argument is Beneath Them, Fair & Just

NEGATIVE

Domineering, Miserly, Bossy, Boastful, Too Materialistic, Shrewd & Cold, Insensitive, Selfish, Looks Down on Others, Indulgent in Foods

The 'eight' is given the power to organize and to lead others. It is the quality of justice and fair play. These people are impartial and unemotional when called upon to make decisions or judgements. They cannot be influenced in their decisions by the emotional displays of others. They are the builders and legislators in a practical world, whose purpose is to establish justice, and to distribute the goods of the earth equitably for the benefit of all. Their sense of personal power makes them fearless when dealing with people on a financial, business or political level. Of course they must be their own boss. They are shrewd in money matters and can account for everything to the last penny, and expect the same accountability from their employees. Organizing others and delegating responsibility is their specialty. They handle large sums of money with ease, and they can spend and borrow with decisiveness and confidence. Too often this quality can use its own sense of power and its financial success exclusively for self-gain. They have a tendency to measure others from a materialistic standpoint. They have a fine appreciation of material values and love the best that money can buy without being ostentatious. They are not emotional. Being cool-headed and objective, they perceive the facts only. It is beneath them to display temper or anger. When unbalanced their sense of power can become misguided and express as a bossy and overly dominant force. They are practical by nature with a good head for figures. Being such a worldly and broad quality, they include a sense of refinement and appreciation for music and the arts as well. Not being naturally endowed with compassion, or a romantic nature, they can find it difficult to be sensitive to the finer touches in a love relationship. To the more sensitive and idealistic types, the 'eight' would appear to be a little too cold and callous. In matters of love they can be quite physically demanding. Their appetites are toward the rich heavy foods. They are quite ambitious, but must learn that to reach the top they must begin at the bottom. Their first and foremost objective is to establish financial independence. This is an accumulative quality that can be quite charitable on the one hand but quite miserly when unbalanced. They are intrigued by high finance and political philosophies. They are basically career-oriented, and so their first priority is business and money, and only then are they concerned with home and family. With so much strength and influence, they must seek the deeper reasons for life and use their leadership ability to establish an equitable and just society. When suffering tension they are affected by generative problems. Women will suffer all forms of female disorders, while the men can be affected through inflammation of the generative organs and other allied problems.

Lesson of the Eight Quality

Learning the lesson of the 'eight' brings a sense of power and well-being. In the gradations of the qualities of two, four and finally into the eight, the lesson has been to understand the potential harmony that exists between one person and another. As we come to understand the spiritual states of the seven, eight and nine we are dealing with a concept of human relations that goes beyond mere personality. Hollywood with its daytime 'soaps,' is an example of the infantile relationship of one person to another when we exist and operate in the realms of personality or *attachment* to our petty egos.

In the eighth stage of mental evolution we have the chance to understand and experience a higher level of connection between peoples. In this higher concept we are not bound by the dictates or morality set by church and state, but by a higher rule that is discovered when the mind is strong enough to sever the bonds of personality. This higher mental order can only be achieved by a profound sense of self-responsibility. We were all meant to experience the deep nurturing element that occurs when two people unite in mind and spirit. This state of union requires absolute openness that can only occur through trust and in the absence of any pretense. We must be able to 'let go.' In other words, we must let go of the ego as it applies to personality and all its foolishness, such as judgements, jealousies and particularly pretentiousness.

The stages of growth from 'one' to 'nine' are all steps leading to the ultimate and detached state of love. In the 'eight,' we are forced to tear ourselves away from an aspect of relationships that is binding and limiting according to the ego's need to possess, control or cling. In the 'eight,' we must reverse the attitude of taking, to one of giving, by tearing this thing called our ego, out of our hearts. If we can accomplish this we begin to understand the cause of temper, irritation, hate, fighting, war and killing. In the 'eight,' we have the chance to learn the lesson of humility through leadership and responsibility to others. If we can accomplish this we can reach the mental state of true objectivity, where our view of others is not from the point of self-measurement but from the point of absolute fairness. From this height, squabbles and altercations between people seem ludicrous because they show two egos in a perpetual struggle to prove the other wrong. It is a never-ending struggle, because where there is egotism there is anger, and where there is anger there is never a solution, only bitterness and alienation.

Why this lesson is so difficult is understood only when the mind grasps the concept of attachment verses detachment. The emotions of one person working through the 'self' or ego are given life, pleasure and enjoyment through the dependence on another. As one person attempts to break that dependence and move into a state of detachment, the egos of both parties can be bruised and hurt. Initially, there are feelings of alienation, fear of loss, guilt and a strong urge to say you're sorry, and then a retreat back into the old familiar relationship. If one is successful in moving into the truly detached or spiritual state, the mind actually comes into a much higher level of love and understanding, but without dependence. It is this separation from one's own ego or selfishness that makes the process so difficult. If you are successful your mind awakens to a far greater sense of your own power for good. Now in the recognition of your own self-control, and mastery of your own temper, there comes the possibility of helping your adversary.

The power of the 'eight' lies in the power to influence another human being. Nothing is quite so satisfying than to see the effect you can have on another's life, of course for their benefit and well-being. In the 'eight' the mind should open up to its potential in leadership, and recognize the power that is really the spirit of life working through the mind when it is truly humble. When we have controlled our moods, irritations and temper there will be power. This power will naturally emerge as the mind loses its desire to hurt or react uncontrollably. It is the power due to a much larger concept of life. It is the power of mental insight into other minds that can bring such repose into our own.

In the Great Pyramid at Giza, in Egypt, the interior passageway leads to the King's chamber, wherein lies the ultimate treasure, the empty sarcophagus. It was never meant as a coffin but as a symbol of the 'ninth' or final stage of growth or attainment. It suggests the final dissolution of the body and of all gross matter. It represents the invisible or unmanifest spirit of life before form, as it passes through form or life to ultimately escape through growth. This is symbolized through the so-called *empty* sarcophagus without a lid or covering. The point here relates to the step or stage prior to the entrance into the King's chamber, or the 'nine.' This is the ante-chamber, and from the ante-chamber the initiate must get down on their hands and knees, with head bowed in order to pass under the low opening before being received into the King's chamber. You understand then the lesson of the 'eight' is the lesson of power through humility. The great power of life manifests through leadership, and leadership is fraught with the possibility of abuse. Humility leads the mind to the realization of simplicity, and the desire to be very ordinary. At the same time we become profoundly aware of the need to serve others, and particularly our intimates who often represent our greatest test and also our greatest opportunity for advancement.

Why do we fight and argue with one another? Because we want to be understood, respected, taken seriously or to just prove a point. In our immature state, we try to do this through shouting or even injuring others in order to force them to accept our point of view. In our attempt to be understood we can become so frustrated that we lose control over our emotions or mind. If we have a shred of intelligence we should realize the insanity of using force or anger to win approval or to resolve conflicts in our personal lives, in politics or on a global level. It is pure egotism that provokes us into abusing others, believing or hoping that this is the only way to gain approval of our ideas. It is simply our ignorance that fosters such behavior.

Shouting at each other has become a way of life. We see it in the political arena, in business dealings and in sports. It demonstrates a complete lack of understanding of how to achieve anything worthwhile. We may force people to accept our ideas and produce change by the very power of our negative force, but there will be no growth, only suppression, which will emerge later to undo us. Anger is absolutely counter-productive and invokes the profound rule of action and reaction. This senseless behavior merely perpetuates the anger and the agony. Those with any kind of conscience will feel shame and remorse at these outbursts of temper.

Temper emerges in consequence of a deep repression and unhappiness. It stems from not being understood. Perhaps most of us know this but seem powerless to change or control these emotional displays in our lives. The point here is that anger is the subtle and sole reason why we cannot have meaningful relationships, and why there is so little beauty and harmony in marriages or on a larger global level. When anger is aroused towards another, our own mind is poisoned and we automatically alienate them . After a while we build such a case against someone it becomes impossible to correct. No amount of counseling or attempts at communication could possibly help. Henceforth, the case becomes larger and larger until the mind becomes obsessed and it thinks of nothing else but how it will justify its case against the other. The mind in this state is so colored by the negative emotion it can only think thoughts that will further its own case. When there is no power of mind to think fairly and objectively, our egotism takes over and directs the show. At this point, we are on an irreversible course where reconciliation is impossible. The result is alienation and separation, and we wander around looking for someone else that will understand us. We may continue to seek consolation by pouring out the sordid details of how we were mistreated or misunderstood, and so we dig ourselves deeper into the hole. It is like the 'ancient mariner,' whose guilt for shooting the albatross is only assuaged by relating his sordid tale to anyone he can. He seeks to do penance, not knowing that unconsciously he perpetuates his own self-pity. So it is when we are not guided by the light of truth, we are influenced by a negative condition that works through our mind.

If we are ever going to solve the problem of conflict individually or collectively, we must see it as a weakness of our own mind. If we insist on seeing the problem as separate from ourselves we will discuss the problem forever and never see the futility of fighting. We must realize that we can start changing a person's attitude toward us by first changing ours towards them.

Self-inquiry is a discipline or a process of the mind turning inward to look at itself and its motivations with scrupulous and impartial honesty and being completely steadfast to a principle.

If the lessons in association are to be learned and we are to cease fighting each other we must begin with the principle of 'no blame' and a kindly thought toward our adversary. 'No blame' has been a part of some of the Oriental philosophies since ancient times. It can be used here to make my point more easily than its Christian equivalent 'no judgement,' because not judging can be construed as meaning that we have no right to evaluate others, when we certainly do.

My aim here is to define a process that is a prerequisite to a more spiritual perspective regarding our relationship with each other. This entails passing through an emotional condition created by our own egotism. It means confronting what I might call the 'phantom' or a negative creation of our own mind. This condition or phantom is very real and powerful and does not want to give up its position or hold within our mind. If there is to be victory over this negative force it can only be because we live by a principle of 'no blame.' If we lose, then we will live to continue the confusion and hostility that is a product of always blaming others for our misery.

Let me be more explicit. In a personal dispute with our intimates for example, where the emotions are aroused, the tendency is to react on the level of the emotional intensity, with the equivalent blame, usually as a defensive mechanism. This is followed by the abusive language, anger and then the remorse, followed by the apologies and the tears, and the resolution never to do it again, at least until the next episode. Fighting and arguing and then attempting to reconcile the situation through the need to communicate our negative feelings to one another, is just an exercise in emotionalism. Emotionalism is a condition of egotism, and the ego will always seek to perpetuate the fight through playing with the emotions over who is right and who is wrong. If this vicious cycle is to end, then the urge to injure another person in word or deed must stop. In the midst of the emotion the mind must turn inward and consider what is happening. It must draw away from the urge to strike back, and be silent. The voice that cries 'no blame' can only be heard in the silence. At this stage, the mind will not know what to do. It must remain in the silence, or resist the urge to strike out for as long as it takes to gain an insight into what must be learned and what is actually going on. This may take a moment of time or it may take months or years, but there is a chance here to build a new aspect to one's character.

This retrenching from the urge to react in anger will be played out again and again, until an insight is gained and the power over one's own destructive emotional nature is realized. Slowly, or in an instant, we can face our 'phantoms' and loosen their power over us and then see them dissolve before our eyes. Then we will understand the struggle that goes on universally with all human beings. In the early stages of this battle we may feel the force of our own negativity as it registers through our nervous system and our body. The first impulse in resisting the urge to strike out is numbness. If we can stay there for even a moment of time without giving into anger, we will begin to see that there is really no need to defend ourselves ever again.

Why this experience is so difficult is because our relationship with our opponent must change radically and therein lies the fear and the flight back to what seems comfortable. If we can continue to resist the urge to react and thus remain quiet, there will be a growing awareness of an emerging spiritual force which is our own divine nature. We will see that no one has the right to abuse anyone. At this point, we will have the strength to stand back, impervious to any destructive criticisms, because we will know the truth of the situation. The right of knowledge or insight is given to those who have conquered their own lower natures. This is because real thinking begins at this point. We have become steadfast in our convictions. Our thinking is no longer influenced by emotion and self-interest. Our relationship with all people at this point will undergo a transformation that will move us beyond personality. This is not desirable to the mass of humanity because it does not feed the ego.

Gaining control over our emotions is not a matter of suppressing anything or remaining passive in order to avoid conflict. On the contrary, now that we are in control we can be firm and confrontational. We can be silent or indifferent when necessary. We can debate and never be pulled into argument. We are becoming teachers because of our awakening sense of responsibility to others. There is no longer any great urge to 'fight to be heard'; instead our motive has changed to consideration toward our adversary. The impulse to blame has been replaced with the power to teach.

To have gained the position of authority by virtue of our kindness, our knowledge and our growing sense of responsibility toward others has automatically earned us the right to leadership. The quality of leadership grows gradually and is self-evident when you discover that people are following you because they choose to. The greatest power that a human being can possess is the power to influence others, with consideration of the admonition, "If the blind lead the blind they all fall into the ditch." Leadership has nothing to do with being domineering. The power of leadership is simply acquired through overcoming our tempers. If this idea is difficult to accept, then challenge yourself with that task. What you will discover if you succeed will astonish you.

The first thing that becomes apparent when a level of emotional control is established is a greater sense of objectivity and awareness of people's intentions and motivations, as well as an expanded consciousness of the meaning of life. Consequently, the urge is awakened to lead others to the same understanding. The world today is almost devoid of spiritual leaders. They are absolutely non-existent in politics, business or orthodox religious institutions. Mohandas K. Ghandi was probably the last political leader the world will see for a long time that was truly concerned for the spiritual well-being of humanity. The rest are almost totally concerned with things practically useless to the preservation of life and spiritual progress. People of substance have long ago withdrawn from the public or political arena as a place where they could work for constructive and effective change.

Leadership deals with power and influence but particularly offers the opportunity for spiritual growth. Spiritual or mental growth does not take place through isolating ourselves from life and escaping to a wilderness where we can contemplate God. Leadership affords the opportunity to contemplate and realize our divinity, and has the potential to awaken us to our responsibilities and to honesty. There is no greater privilege than being a leader. In leadership there is more freedom to govern your own time, to help others, to travel, to acquire wealth and particularly to know and understand spiritual power. It is only in leadership that we can come to know the spiritual force as it expresses through us when our efforts are directed toward "the greatest good for the greatest number." While it is humbling to be a good follower, it is infinitely more rewarding to be a good leader. If we aspire to spirituality, we must desire to become a leader and to learn what leadership can teach us.

The urge to lead is inherent in all people, although it is stronger in some. It awakens more fully when we become accomplished at something that eventually propels us into leadership by virtue of our knowledge and our expertise. Now we must distinguish between what we 'think' we know and what we actually know. The difference is expressed as either benevolence and kindness, or as dominance and cruelty.

Leadership provides privilege and the power to influence others. Leadership draws others to itself. Those who look for a leader subordinate themselves, and are then open to be led, and herein lies the privilege and power that the leader feels. If the leader abuses the privilege they lose the power. If they acknowledge the responsibility, they gain respect and discover what a great privilege it is to serve others.

To use our power to acquire wealth at the expense of an ignorant and suppressed 'labor force' is the worst kind of tyranny. I'm not suggesting we have to share equally all things that are produced, including profits, but only to consider that the "laborer is worthy of his hire." On the other hand the laborer who remains subordinate for too long never comes to know their own power.

We must gain the power to first move ourselves away from useless jobs standing on assembly lines, pushing paper around in offices or engaging in other occupations too numerous to mention, that are soul-destroying. The system we now live in will disintegrate when people refuse to support it or to become slavishly subservient to it. As I have said before, it only requires that we become creative to the point of realizing our individuality and doing something useful in life.

The power to lead comes when we acquire the ability to see intelligently into others' eyes and to see where they are and what their needs are. The world desperately needs leaders who have vision, wisdom and the courage to tackle the real problem concerning human behavior. When we can make a distinction between a life that supports self-interest and that which is spiritually motivated, then we can lead the battle towards reform.

In the highest sense becoming a leader is not an arbitrary decision. You do not decide you want to be a leader. Leadership occurs through a process of detachment. Some are ready for this great task, and are chosen and forced to deal with that element that will separate them from their grosser passions, to allow for true objectivity. If they pass the test, they enter into a place of calmness and emotional stability where there is objectivity and a dispassionate view of all problems.

When we can truly begin to understand the meaning of "being our brother's keeper," we will become responsible in our involvement with each other in the same way that a mother cares for her child. It is at this juncture that the mind begins to move away from a self-oriented focus. If the power to help our intimates is awakened instead of anger or intolerance, we begin the transformation from one mental state to an entirely new one. In this transition, the mind begins to understand the difference between a life that is primarily motivated by selfishness, and one where the spirit of truth is becoming apparent. Now we can stand in the midst of the conflict with a confidence in our 'inner consciousness,' knowing that we will do or say the right thing, because our responses are not coming from a self-centered point of view. We are beginning to really care about others. The mind can begin to feel the impulse from its true source or from 'within.' In the merging with our true self, we are becoming an *individual*. We are now becoming aware of a purpose or the meaning behind the many experiences in our life. Everything we do from now on must have meaning. There can be no waste of time. There can be no serving of 'two masters,' only the one. No matter how obscure the path may seem at times, there is no loss of confidence because a commitment has been made to serve life and others. There is a motivation that is almost inexplicable.

There can be no awareness of the higher aspects of life if any steps toward self-mastery have been left out. The mastery of the passions depends on control of temper and moods. A strong intellect demands a discipline over emotional indulgences of every kind. Worry and fear must be expunged and their origins understood. In gaining our independence, we can never be subservient to another human being. We must be free of loneliness through our deep communion with others. All these lessons and many more must be learned before the mind can awaken this sense of 'responsibility.' If we can reach this point, then there is a shift in our consciousness. Now we can begin to understand our unique position in the overall picture of life. We can see our specific role and we know what we have to do. This insight of our individual destiny has grown out of our accomplishments and our desire to add something to the sum total of human progress.

As we come to distinguish between ego response and spirit response, we will understand the meaning of 'detachment.' That is, we have no dependence on anything or anyone. At this point, there is no one that can help us any longer. Even if there is a lingering urge to be helped, deep inside of yourself you know that you are beyond being helped. It is pointless to cry out to our gods because the cry reverberates as the voice of self-pity. Worship is useless because it is in denial of one's own divinity, and prayer is the noise that cries out in despair in order to avoid the silence. At this point the mind must stand alone, able finally to draw from its own spiritual resources.

When we move beyond the problematic state, it becomes easy to see that religion and modern psychology have focused on sympathy with the 'problem,' rather than with the 'spirit.' Thus, it has always been the wise only who can tell the difference between a symptom and the true cause of a problem. Counselors and teachers invariably make the mistake of catering to a person's problem and consequently fail to awaken the force of love or compassion.

In my own research on the nature of the Chakras there is no mention of the names of any Chakras beyond the seventh, but there is definitely a reference to their existence. The number eight represents the final goal in our relationship with each other through the evolutionary steps beginning with the 2, then the 4 and finally the 8. Our link in other words to this state of inward peace and power is through a deep and profound union or surrender to another soul.

To have governed our emotional responses, or to simply have controlled our temper, brings the mind to a place of peace and power. This happens to the few who do not seek power, but who have withstood the test, and then have become aware of their influence on others. These few seek to serve, not to control. They can meet force with force and expose evil for what it is. This is justice.

Now we are ready to enter into the final stage or step toward the experience of love. In other words we must come to know the difference between passion and compassion. The former usually ends up serving the ego while the latter serves the soul.

Nine

Positive	**Negative**
Universal Love, Inspirational, Idealistic, Sympathetic, Artistic, Loves to Help Others, Compassionate, Specialist, Intuitive, Dramatic, Loves all People, Generous, Spiritual Teacher	Self-Pity, Too Emotional, Loss of Temper, Impractical, Over-Sexed & Indulgent in the Emotions, Fanatical, Psychic, Complainer, Suffer Extreme Highs & Lows, Depressed

The 'nine' represents the highest expression of the life force through sound, wisdom and the spoken word. It is the purpose of the 'nine' to rise above sense dependence and to teach humanity the way of life. People with 'nines' are imbued with love and compassion for all humanity. This is an inspirational force that awakens the feeling of love and allows us to see the basic good in all of humanity. Those with 'nines' respond sympathetically to suffering, whether to people, plants or animals. Through sympathy and caring, they establish links with people that create trust and openness. Thus, they become the spiritual teachers, administering to the needs of others through love and understanding. Their love can be full of caring and tenderness. This is an artistic and creative force, but very emotional when it is undeveloped or undisciplined. They can swing from the extremes of inspiration to the depths of despair. They can be drawn to religions, philosophies or occult studies in their search for the meaning of their lives. Because of their deeply religious nature they can be drawn into all forms of psychic phenomena and must guard against becoming fanatical. The 'nines' are the most giving and caring of all the qualities. They know just how to please others, even in the smallest things. In choosing gifts, they seem to know just what you would like, and sometimes they will spare no expense. They will literally give you the shirt off their back. They are called upon to give over and over again. Their love of people is meant to be of the very highest, and when it becomes too personal they tend to lose that which they cling to or become possessive of. They have a fear of losing things, and this overwhelming fear can sometimes draw them into tragic circumstances. They can become the most jealous and demanding lovers. When unbalanced, they can suffer outbursts of temper which can literally destroy their lives. Because of the intensity of their feelings it can sometimes take years to get over personal losses. Self-pity is their greatest challenge. If they cannot develop their intellect, they will be ruled by their feelings and suffer the perverse results of becoming sense dependent. They are quite sexual and must learn to understand the love force as it manifests through the passions, as well as through the intellect. They are easily lifted to the highest, through music or drama and are deeply moved by plays or operas dealing with tragedy. They need to work or express in areas where they are dealing with people, where they can help and serve them. The 'nine' includes all other numbers and is a specialist and a perfectionist in many different fields, but still works best in some humanitarian pursuit. They do not enjoy hard physical work or routine domestic responsibilities. Their love shines through their eyes, and they are at their best when they are inspiring others. In the highest, their compassion and love has a magnetism that draws others to them. This is one of the more difficult paths to follow because they must sacrifice the lower and exemplify the higher, in order to become revelators of wisdom. Through emotional indulgence and tension they are affected through their whole nervous system. They can be afflicted by anything from minor nervous disorders to total nervous breakdowns.

Explanation of the Nine Quality

Having become detached in the 'eight' or impersonal in our relationships with others, gives us license to move out into life to love and serve all people. The three, six, and finally the nine are gradations or stages of our potential ascent from the love of passionate connection, on through to the higher aspects of love as experienced in the feeling of compassion and spiritual connection.

In the 'nine' we can come to feel and experience the power of love through the physical and emotional channel, or we can experience that same love, devoid of the sexual implication as we link through dialogue. The unique characteristic common to all humans is a sophisticated potential use of language. It is language that gives the very meaning and purpose to the mind of man and woman. It is in our dialogue or conversation with each other that either love or hate can arise. It has been said that the power behind love manifests through sound and the spoken word, but only when it is deep and profound and comes forth as wisdom. In earlier times it was written that, "When two or more are gathered together in *my* name, so am *I* there also." This suggests that when the conversation between people is deep and profound, the 'I,' which represents the power of life itself, is present and felt by the participants taking part in the discussion of life.

In the earlier stages of the evolution through numbers, we came to understand the necessity of overcoming the ego or selfishness of our intentions. Now we can come to realize that if our intentions are in consideration of others' needs, conversation can awaken a deep or soul connection. The 'nine' represents the power of the teacher expressing wisdom. All our efforts in life are ultimately leading us to share and to give of ourselves through the spoken word. To be understood and loved by others brings life's greatest satisfaction. Of course we must be found worthy of love and of being listened to. This is the lesson of the 'nine.' If we have passed through all the previous lessons successfully, true speech or wisdom awakens and expresses through us spontaneously, and then there is love. Before this, we are found grasping for it, demanding it from others and even beating others when they refuse to honor us.

Life gives us our opportunity to taste of the beauty of love quite early as we enter the period of puberty. It arises alongside, or in conjunction with sexual arousal of the opposites, male and female. Love and sexual arousal are separate elements. The one can lead to the other, or the one can be bypassed for the sake of the other, depending upon the maturity and wisdom of the couples. In either case, love awakens when two people surrender themselves in heart and mind to each other. In one case, the power of love arises alongside the sexual opening, while in the other it can be opened through the right dialogue. In both cases there must be complete surrender to, and acceptance of the other.

In the 'nine' we are closer to our true purpose in giving and serving life, and therefore closer to the opportunity to enter into communion or a dialogue that can open us to a love experience. Love is the power of life expressing itself through a person as he or she pursues meaning and purpose. When two people come together in dialogue which is devoid of pretense, in the absence of self-serving motives, there will naturally be a certain spark created. Love is not very difficult to awaken within oneself, but it is very difficult to sustain without great intelligence and wisdom. Love is easy to pursue through the physical channel. The danger there is in losing the sacredness of that experience through an indulgence in sex.

It is a rare condition in the history of men and women to find or create love through the development of wisdom, and through a deep and profound mental intimacy. It is the total submission or subjugation to the spiritual force, through a completely selfless existence or devotion to life, that opens the mind to the *teacher* within or to *speech*. The rule of the teacher is not to demand subordination or subservience of anyone, but to be the example and to merely inspire the pupil with wisdom and truth. Devotion to the teacher or any other idol or image, living or dead, may produce a momentary experience of sublime love, but in consequence could bind the student to a perpetual subordination to the living or dead image. In so doing, the student may sacrifice their own growth, and an ultimate recognition of their own divinity.

What we are all seeking in the 'nine' is compassion. Compassion is a deep and open-hearted response to the suffering of others. The question I ask is, do we feel this response as a sympathy to the suffering, or for the spirit of the individual struggling for expression? Do we merely cater to their problem or have we the power to help them? Do we support their problematic state or do we teach them? Does the sufferer want to be helped or just sympathized with?

To illustrate this point I will relate an experience which was a turning point in my own life. Like so many others on a spiritual quest, my problems were such that I felt strongly that I needed someone to help me. I could not seem to reach beyond a certain point. I was not happy with much of my life, even though I had practiced a multitude of disciplines in an endeavor to contact something higher. I did not realize that in my problematic state I was really 'outward seeking' although I could not see it at the time. I was lost in 'self.' I could not seem to solve my problems by myself no matter how much of a stoic I assumed I was. All my efforts at 'turning inward' proved futile.

There happened to be a man that had come into my life that proved to be wise and loving. At first I could not understand why he gave me such a rough time whenever I tried to pull him into a debate on certain philosophical points. Even though he gave me a difficult time, I was bound to him for some inexplicable reason. Part of this was the love emanating from his eyes as well as a sensing of his great intelligence. One day when I had reached the end of my rope and I was fit to be tied, I surrendered what I thought was my pride and I went to see this wonderful man. By this time I was desperate. He welcomed me into his home and I sat down and began to pour out my anguish. He listened for maybe a minute or two then stood up, made a comment about my stupidity and left through the front door and left me sitting there in his home, alone and totally dejected.

This man forced me to face my self-pity. I finally realized that my previous efforts of turning inward for spiritual guidance were really a subtle and disguised exercise in turning outward for sympathy. There is nothing so all-consuming as self-pity. We can spend our entire life wallowing in it. It is at the moment when our mind can move beyond the influence of self-pity that its true power begins to be recognized. The way this man dealt with my preoccupation with my problems may seem peculiar, but for me it worked wonders. We subsequently made a much deeper connection which allowed both of us to express ourselves more deeply and freely.

We must come to know and experience the difference between a positive thought, and a negative one that becomes a mental interference. The former condition recognizes the power of one's own divinity while the latter state doubts it.

The power we call compassion is the power of love itself. Compassion is the profound sensation of love when there is complete trust and openness. This is the prerequisite for the expression of wisdom from the teacher to the pupil, or for that matter between any two people.

So it is when male and female come together via the passions. The love force is awakened because of the complete surrender to each other. In both cases there is a total giving into each other of body, mind and soul. With the passions there is a strong tendency towards ego gratification, while compassion awakens the power to serve and an awareness that we are only instruments of the spiritual force. The more we serve the more access we have to that force.

All the Holy books of the earth have related the timeless struggle of the human race to evolve beyond the preoccupation with the passions. If we have no experience with the 'higher' we will always be pulled back to the 'lower.' Theories abound to justify our need to explore our sexuality as a means of reaching deeper into our relationship with our partners. Nothing could be further from the truth. Complications within the sexual aspects of an individual reflect a confused mind.

The chance to awaken this spiritual power through the mind becomes known when we cease taking and begin giving. This is the path of the teacher. The teacher desires to be stimulated intellectually and spiritually, rather than physically through the genitals. The very spirit of the individual can be awakened through mental communion, but only when the union is deep enough. "Love is understanding." There is only one basic reason for coming together with anyone and that is to share in the inquiry of life. When this inquiry reaches into deeper and deeper levels, the spirit can actually be touched and the feeling of it can be shared by the participants. The feeling is of love and affection for all. There is no need or desire for sexual stimulation.

At this point, the mind begins to see the difference between reality and illusion. In other words the glamour and charm of sense-stimulating experiences such as sex begin to wear thin. We see that it has been a problem of our loneliness and basic frustration with life. The mind begins to see that it has been used, that its desires have been illusory or conjured up by the imagination.

In the perception of truth, the mind discovers its own creative potential. The senses are now free from distortion and capable of a deep response to all of the beauty of life, including a deeper union with those who would dare to open to us.

It is a tragedy to observe people coming together every day of their lives and unconsciously avoiding the possibility of deep communion with each other. The chance to acquaint ourselves with the very soul of another human being is usually avoided through the fear and immaturity of our mind and desires. Every day we are given the opportunity to enter deeply into the pleasure of another's company for the purpose of becoming spiritually intimate. Instead, our conversations will usually end up being pointless expressions of years of practiced pretentiousness. We can carry out this charade throughout our entire lives and never be conscious of the missed opportunity for that soul connection with another mind.

If speech is empowered by wisdom the mind is enlivened. The spiritual force is carried on a current of sound. This is why a singer or orator can inspire their audience to great heights if the proper connection with the audience is made, but only if the performer is inspired. All then, will experience the uplifting presence of 'spirit.'

The real power behind speech begins to awaken around puberty and is called emotion. In the truly mature adult the power of speech expresses itself through wisdom and is awakened through compassion. Nothing should be spoken without great consideration to its consequences. No thought once expressed can ever be recalled. To suppress the urge to speak, in order to consider our intent is a good discipline. A teacher speaks not to impress but to inform, not to coerce but to stimulate. Our consciousness expands more rapidly as we realize our intent for every word spoken. Intent reveals wisdom or its absence.

The possibility for spiritual advancement applies mostly to those who search out ways for sharing their degree of wisdom. Religions and philosophies stagnate if their members do not go out to impart what wisdom they have learned. In fact the mind is *compelled* to share its own discoveries and to find ways of doing so. If there are no discoveries the mind atrophies and the spirit withdraws. This is the reason religions die and become empty shells, and their shouts, rants and revivals become hollow reverberations reflecting their emptiness.

Speech should arise out of the silence, not from the emotions. When it comes from the stillness of inquiry it has power. When it is from the emotions it is usually babble. When it is merely self-expression it is heard and forgotten in a moment. Only truth is everlasting so that the mind that merges with spirit or truth begins to understand the concept of 'everlasting life.'

If we desire to be spiritual and to find peace of mind we must acquire the ability to help others. If we desire to be teachers we must awaken the power to *speak*. We become teachers when we have something to say. We become more spiritual when our speech is discreet and inspired by compassion and directed by wisdom

To teach is inherent in everyone. It is the final goal. Initially we shout, rant and rave to be heard and to be understood. The feeling of being understood ultimately comes when we have learned the great lessons as illustrated in such thoughts as, "casting our pearls before swine" or "letting the dead bury the dead."

Self or egotism lives and thrives through the emotions. All problems have their existence through the emotions. A problem is only a problem because we feel it as such, although it originates in the mind. All problems are expressions of self or a form of egotism. They exist because of a self-inflicted sadness through self-pity. In other words, when we cannot get what we want we cry about it, blame others and generally feel miserable. Our ego is born and grows through our selfishness. Giving is the way of the spirit, while taking is the path of the ego.

Ego flourishes through emotionalism in avenues that are profoundly subtle. The ego can bind or trap the mind through sex stimulation, affection, music and the many other emotional and self-satisfying pursuits. In themselves these pursuits are not wrong, but as the mind develops, it must be able to make a distinction between enjoying these things for their own sake, and craving them for the gratification of the ego. If we are very astute we will see that behind the need for affection, for instance, there is an ego lurking and needing to be stroked. When the mind becomes a little wise it can begin to feel and see the mischief wrought, for example, in the sensation of sexual arousal and its potential for familiarity. This does not make sexual arousal wrong or bad.

Every problem originates in the mind through improper concepts and wrong thinking. All incorrect thoughts register their results in the emotions and our feelings. "The thought is always father to the deed." When the mind grows sufficiently to understand this, it begins to make a distinction between the deeper aspect of itself called spirit, and the superficial element that it has allowed to grow, called ego. They are separate elements of the one mind that define the struggle or spiritual journey through life.

Compassion is the profound feeling that is generated between one soul and another soul. This represents two people united in spirit where problems do not enter into the picture. The run of humanity are caught in the emotional reactions of sympathy and self-pity, which could be viewed as the soap-opera drama of life.

'Self' or ego feeds on and expresses through desire or sense stimulation. Ego is kept alive through loneliness, sorrow, fear of losing friends and things, jealousy, possessiveness and a host of other fears. When the mind is united in spirit it can endure the void and inspire itself when there is no one to relate to. Spirit stands alone and is self-satisfied. A spiritual mind has found the joy of thinking and seeks only to teach, not to feed on others.

In the East the concept of detachment defines the ordeal of moving away from the ego's need for recognition and dependence on others, or sympathy and support of any kind. If the ordeal can be endured, the mind begins to open up to clear thinking, thinking that is not clouded by hidden agendas and subtle fears which are ego-motivated. This task is almost impossible for most people that have become sense dependent, because any effort toward self-discipline awakens the phantoms of the ego and produces symptoms of withdrawal.

These insufferable elements of a person's life are revealed the moment they open their mouth to speak. It is for the wise to respond appropriately and compassionately to all people under all circumstances. In the ninth Chakra, "speech" or the teacher awakens and begins to experience the *power* expressing through the spoken word. There is no more babble. In the lesson of the 3, speech begins its formation and evolves to completion in the 9. There is no greater privilege than the experience of being the revelator of truth, as it emerges spontaneously in an appropriate manner meeting all circumstances. The ninth Chakra or psychic center releases the power of life that energizes and awakens the feeling of total well-being of body and mind. In this state the mind cannot be pulled into its desire nature, because it has found its path and its joy.

The Great Pyramid

Let me illustrate my point by bringing you, in mind, to the Gizeh Plateau, in Egypt. There stands in the complex of buildings and pyramids, the last great wonder of the world, the Great Pyramid. It is a magnificent engineering marvel, as well as a symbol of spiritual significance. The outward measurements of the pyramid have revealed the arithmetical wisdom of the architect. Inwardly it embodies a symbolism that makes known the path of spiritual evolution. It is the eternal story of the surrender of the lower nature to the higher. It is simply illustrated as follows:

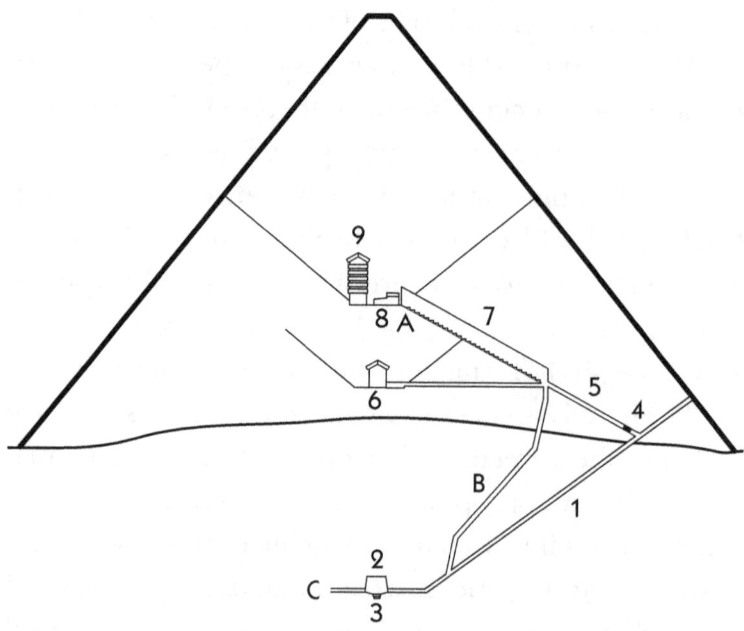

1 **Descending Passageway** – If we do not aspire to discover the meaning to our life we descend to the lower or sub-terranean depths.

2 **Subterranean Chamber** – A rough and unfinished chamber, suggesting an incomplete life, lived out in a subconscious state.

3 **Bottomless Pit** – There is no end to the depths we can fall when the mind becomes obsessed with self-interest.

C **Passageway Leading Nowhere** – When we live for 'self' or in the lower realms, all efforts lead nowhere.

4 **Granite Plug** – If we choose to ascend and find the way upward through purpose, there will always be obstacles that block the way.

5 **Ascending Passageway** – A passage to a 'new life' always exists if we continue to ascend and to raise our minds to higher levels.

B **The Misstep** – Even up to and including the 6th stage the snake of 'self' can still cause us to take a misstep where we end up back in the pit.

6 **Queen's Chamber** – A half complete chamber to signify a partial opening of the mind to its inner consciousness. This signifies self-mastery and individuality.

7 **Grand Gallery** – The first stage into the spiritual domain. An opening of the senses to the grandness of life. At this stage the mind opens to life in awe and gratitude.

A **The Great Step** – If we are to become powerful and influential we must take the great step of overcoming our tempers.

8 **Ante-Chamber** – Now we must prepare to go through an initiation before we are allowed entrance into the King's Chamber. Here we must be humbled.

9 **King's Chamber** – The place where the mind is released from its struggle. Finally speech is awakened as the mind is opened to the wisdom of life.

Life begins with the birth of a child who is unaware of the life process. The child is completely concerned with its own needs, and if not trained, can become totally selfish and descend into the subconscious levels that lead nowhere. The parallel here relates to the *descending* passageway in the pyramid which travels beneath its base and penetrates the bedrock. It then opens out into the first or Subterranean Chamber with its so called 'Bottomless Pit.' From the Subterranean Chamber there is a passageway that was thought to lead to the great treasure, but the intruders found to their surprise that it ended at a dead end, *leading nowhere.* So it is when we are living exclusively for 'self' or in a subconscious state, no matter what new paths we create, they are going to end up going nowhere. If we are going to evolve, we must locate the pathway leading upward, beyond the influence of emotional incentives.

Just short of a hundred feet from its entrance, the ceiling of the descending passage reveals the start of the *ascending* passage. It was originally sealed with a granite slab in order to hide it from the uninitiated. The descending and the ascending passages are about 4 feet high. The ascending passageway just into its entrance is abruptly blocked by a 'Granite Plug,' as it is called. It is slightly tapered and wedged into the passageway. With extreme effort, it could be pushed or pulled back and removed from the passage. The Granite Plug symbolizes the test or the challenge ahead of us, if we choose to conquer our weaknesses and continue to ascend.

Everything we do is tested at some point for its logic and its continuation. Our undertakings and perceptions of life will either move us forward or become our nemesis. We are exposed to our faults in the four period or cycle. If we choose to evolve or ascend, we must remove the plugs or blocks in our path. Moving beyond difficulties requires in-depth concentration, study and thought, which seems beyond the average person.

The 1, 2 and 3 in their negative expression relate to 'self' and a downward slide. The 4, 5 and 6 provide the opportunity to grow and continue upward, where much effort must be put forth with very little result showing. If we are able to remove the 'plug,' we can continue to climb the narrow ascending passageway. Now, the upper end of the first stage of the ascending passage ends and provides an option of resting and going off along a horizontal passageway, or continuing our climb upward into the 'Grand Gallery.' The natural thing to do is to investigate the horizontal passage first, which is called the Queen's Passage, which leads to the Queen's Chamber. As you step into this narrow passage, there is an opening in the floor which according to archeologists is a "strange" and even narrower passage. It drops almost straight down out of sight and joins up with the descending passage, and then back into the Subterranean Chamber, with its Bottomless Pit. This passage they say, "starts with a torn and ragged opening which bores irregularly and somewhat tortuously down through the masonry to the descending passage, far below the ground level." The message here suggests that even up to this point, there is always the possibility of taking a misstep and falling back and losing our hold on life and the growth process. If we can avoid the pitfall leading along the narrow passage, we enter into the 'sixth' stage or Queen's Chamber, which we discover is only half complete.

It is interesting to note that the three Chambers on the three levels within the pyramid have a distinct difference. The Subterranean Chamber is completely unfinished and dug out of the rough bedrock. The walls of the Queen's Chamber are rough and only half of them are highly polished granite, while the King's Chamber is complete in every respect. So it is in life, there is no reward or completion until the concept is complete and the final step taken.

When the archeologists were first exploring the Great Pyramid, the theory was that the builders changed their minds as to where to place the dead Pharaoh's body. The location of the chambers then changed to higher and higher locations until they decided on the King's Chamber. As a point of fact, it is well to note that "there has never been found an original burial in any of the pyramids in Egypt," which suggests that the Pyramids were never built as tombs in the first place.

If we can stay in the process and continue the climb along the Grand Gallery, which is an extension of the ascending passage continuing up at the same angle, we get to view a magnificent part of these corridors and chambers. It is almost 30 feet high and was constructed of highly polished granite. It is said, "The glory of the workmen who built the Great Pyramid, is in the masonry of the Grand Gallery." This represents the beginning of the harvest time of our effort as our mind enters into the spiritual domain, or the number 7.

As we climb to the end of the Grand Gallery we come to the Great Step. As an aside, I find it interesting that the names of these different chambers, passageways and parts of the interior structure have been, by chance, so appropriately named by the archeologists, as they struggled upward through the passages. The height of the Great Step is approximately 3 feet. In other words, if we choose to continue our upward journey, we must take the next step which is a Great one. This implies the control of one's temper. As this is accomplished, the mind begins to understand the true meaning of power and influence. This control brings an awareness of the power to help others.

The Ante-Chamber with its low entrance way into the King's Chamber is the final and most difficult lesson. Only on our knees, with our head bowed could we gain entrance to the King's Chamber. The Great Step and the low entrance to the Kings Chamber relate to the lessons of the '8.' It is the lesson of submission and humility wherein we learn to put others before ourselves. Finally we are led to the 9 and to an awareness that permits us to see ourselves as we truly are and were meant to be. The walls of the King's Chamber are all constructed of highly polished granite. The ceiling is covered by 9 huge granite beams. Inside this chamber, as I have previously mentioned is a lidless, 'empty,' granite rectangular box or Sarcophagus. Sarcophagi have been found in other pyramids throughout Egypt and they have *all* been *empty*, even those pyramids that have never been previously entered since their inception. In the story of Jesus Christ's burial in the tomb we find that on the third day he had "risen" and disappeared. The story relates to the final attainment or ascension wherein we "sit upon the right hand of God the Father," completely free at last. We have finally escaped from the wheel of life no longer to reincarnate, as they say in the East. We have learned all our lessons and have merged with the eternal truth which opens the mind to the expression of wisdom.

This magnificent building or stone edifice is a record of the wisdom that is embodied without and within its structure. Throughout the world there are similar structures that embody the same message. In South East Asia there are a number of 9 stage temples built in another age. When the caretakers or Buddhist monks are questioned as to their meaning, the reply is, "The 9 stages represent the steps the Buddha took to gain enlightenment. The first three relate to the physical, the second three to the mental and the final three to the spiritual plane." In Central America the jungle is full of ancient Mayan ruins. Most of them are built in 3 or 9 stages as a reference to the trinity or principle of thirds. In Tikal, the main Temple Pyramid is built with 9 stages or levels with 90 steps leading to the top. It is not well known that the ancient Mayans, like the Egyptian Pharaohs, changed their names and understood the changing cycles from 1 through 9.

And so it is that the mind evolves through the lessons inherent within the numbers from 1 through 9. There is no magic about mental or spiritual evolution. It is a gradual process as we extract the lessons of life from our experiences, in our efforts to contribute something useful to life. There is nonetheless a *master key* which is the knowledge that pertains to a balanced name. To see a child who has been given a balanced name from birth, demonstrates the value of this principle. There are no guarantees promising wisdom and happiness. The balanced name serves as the vehicle only.

CHAPTER THREE

Sample Analysis of Marlon Brando

The following analysis is a very brief demonstration of how the individual qualities of a person's character, when mixed together through the names and birthdate, create the overall personality, with its strengths and weaknesses. I have chosen the popular and talented actor Marlon Brando because he stands out as a dominant force in the entertainment industry and he is someone that most of us know through the movies.

	7		7	5
Marlon	3	**Brando**	2	5
	1		9	1
Birthdate – April		3	1924	
4		3	7 – 5	

The following is a brief and sample analysis showing the combined influences of the first and last name, the two names combined, as well as the influences of the birthdate [month, day, year] of the life of Marlon Brando, born on April 3, 1924.

I will begin the analysis by relating the inward or forces of inclination, as defined through his month, day and year of birth. In other words his true path is represented by the lessons of his birth date. If he is going to be fulfilled in life, it is these inward influences or lessons that must be learned and expressed through his endeavors.

Remember that it is the degree of *balance* within the *name* that determines the success or failure of one's life. In other words the individual qualities in our total makeup are either expressed in their highest and positive sense, or in their lowest and negative sense, or perhaps a bit of both.

Being born on April 3, 1924, makes Marlon Brando a 5 in the major life position. He therefore has the potential to become a reformer in life because he feels strongly the pretense and the injustice within society at large, as well as within any individual in his company. The 5 will have created a deep restlessness within him which originates in the need to find the meaning, purpose and truth within his experiences. His early awareness will be of the sham and the artificiality of people around him, which will prompt him to challenge them and ultimately awaken the urge to right the wrongs of humanity. At least that is his potential purpose. Whether the 5 in his true nature is expressed in the highest or lowest is of course dependent upon the balance or imbalance of the name. In the highest it will awaken an enormous drive and challenging nature, that will respond to any injustice or untruth by attempting to expose it. In the lowest the 5 can express as an enormous frustration and compel him to come out fighting against any and all forms of repression, simply for the satisfaction of putting others down.

Marlon can live to be a true reformer or merely a rebel at odds with life, or a little bit of both. The 5 is a powerful force that can be used for good or evil depending upon whether it is directed intelligently or otherwise. It is for the 5 to expose the rot and corruption of life as well as the outworn dogmas that stay the progress of humanity. Only the 5 has the courage and the potential intellect capable of perceiving the error in the ways of others and then confronting it. They will always side with the underdog. They are spurred on by a challenge, and in the midst of the fight they must find the truth and then they cannot lose. The search for truth has always been the motive force in this man's life. The 5 is a very independent force, versatile and changeable, that must not be suppressed. It represents 'new life.' It is a powerfully creative force when it is motivated by a cause, and terribly destructive when lacking a noble idealism. The downside of this quality is in the restlessness that can cause premature changes and incomplete projects because of boredom. Any weakness surrounding the 5 will affect him in the solar plexus and the stomach. He could be prone to ulcers.

The first minor lesson of 4, from the month of April compelled him as a boy to pursue his interests with a focus towards perfection and detail. This influence allows him to persevere with the things that he loves, and gives him a strong practical approach to his endeavor. The 4 also produces a strong physical side to his character.

Now the other major influence from his birthdate relates to the *day* of his birth which is 3, and this puts him into the air or inspirational grouping. This inspirational side to his nature through the birth day of 3 makes him a basically emotional character type, with the potential to inspire others. Again, this influence can express in high creative endeavor or simply through emotional indulgence. Which way it expresses depends upon the degree of fulfillment through balance, or the proper correlation of all his influences. Being in the air group gives him a deep emotional response to his life experiences which makes him a 'natural' as an actor. He is born to entertain and to inspire us through the expression of his deep emotion. Added to this natural depth of emotion are all the 7s in his name. The 7 gives him a great dramatic ability in his character portrayals. The air group quality is motivated by love and humor. The 3 is a very expressive and extroverted quality full of love for all people. The 7s in his name, being the compelling force, move him away from people. The contradiction and play of opposing forces working in this man's life do not make it easy for him. On the one hand there is an enormous need to be demonstrative in his affections, but the 7s create an aloofness and a need for privacy that keeps people at a distance. Nonetheless, the root or basic influence of the air group awakens the urge to experience love and affection either in the highest sense or the basest sense. He is fortunate to have acting as a medium for the expression of so much emotion. He would find it difficult to reconcile the fierce level of independence and privacy due to the names, with his natural magnanimous and happy inner nature as related to the air group. The compelling force of the names will always predominate. As an air group person his potential lies in influencing others through his passion for life and its expression through the power of speech.

The last minor influence from the year of birth,1924, is a 7. This moved into his life around the age of 54. Going from the 3 middle influence, from 27 to 54, to the 7 of the last minor influence from 54 to the end of his life will have produced a dramatic change. He may wonder why it is becoming so easy to accept his withdrawal from people. He will quite enjoy becoming the recluse and delving into creative pastimes where he can indulge himself in reading and even writing his memoirs perhaps. In any case he will enjoy time to himself without having to respond to the demands of others. Now he can dedicate himself to his love of all things in nature and his interest in the more mystical aspect of life.

So far I have mainly dealt with Marlon Brando's potential, or the forces of inclination as defined through the qualities of the birthdate. Now I will deal with the compelling forces as revealed through the names.

First of all I will explain the lesser influence of the surname, which is still very important because it can either detract from the whole character or contribute to it in a positive way.

The surname of Brando is a 7-2-9. Remember it is only the 7 and the 9 that are analyzed. Here we have a name that is deeply sensitive to the deeper aspects of life. Every member of this family is prone to misunderstandings, separations, divorces and losses through the affections. This is because they draw from such a depth of feeling and emotion, which is almost impossible for them to understand, and even more difficult for anyone else that tries to understand them. It is a force that craves to love and be loved, and yet it alienates others through cold moods. There is so much feeling, emotion and mysticism in the combination of the 7 and 9 that it can become a force that is difficult to control and stabilize. They can fluctuate from the extremes of inspiration and love, to the depths of desperation. They are deep and sensitive in their appreciation of nature and of art. They are drawn to religious experiences whether orthodox or otherwise. In Marlon Brando's case I doubt, because of his 5s, that he would have anything to do with conventional religion, but I have no doubt that his experiences in nature could be quite profound. He needs to write in order to define and share his deep thoughts. Because of the 7 which somewhat suppresses the inherent quality of the 3, I would say he is quite a lonely man. The 7-2-9 of the surname does not lend itself to the warmth and pleasantries of home and family, and yet because of the 9, at times he would feel great compassion for his intimates and towards the downtrodden.

The most dominant and compelling force in his life is the first name of Marlon which is a 7-3-1 or a 7 and a 1 influence. Again we have a 7 in the soul position making him a man with great depth of feeling, with the dream of getting away from the crass environments of superficial and small-minded people. The weakness of so much 7 is the response or impulse to judge others too quickly. He would not "tolerate fools gladly." I say this because of the combination of the 5 and 7 in his makeup. Keep in mind that he has a deep love nature, but possessing such dual elements he would have to be very selective in the people he associates with. Remember that the 1, 5 and 7 are the independent numbers or qualities. Marlon Brando is then fiercely independent with a great need of quiet places, away from the confusion of the market place. The 1, 5 and 7 are not social qualities in any way, so Marlon having so many of these numbers would at times be quite unsociable and perhaps at times even anti-social and reclusive. The 1 and 7 are limited in the fluidity of verbal expression. The 1 is candid and honest while the 5 is insightful of your faults. These are not easy qualities to reconcile with the deep inherent love nature from the inner quality of the 3 or air group. Moods are his nemesis because of the predominance of 7 and the inability of the 7 to find the necessary depth of understanding from his intimates. Here is an intelligent man that cannot easily communicate the depth of his feelings to those close to him. To tolerate lesser mentalities is not easy, and he would probably say, not even desirable. The name of Marlon gives him strength, self-confidence and depth, but few of the social graces, that if developed would satisfy the inner potential to influence others through his true love nature. With the qualities in his names he could commune with the forces of nature, but in so doing would withdraw too much into himself, which would tend to make him overly introspective. From childhood he has been a solitary man able to stand alone and make his own way through life, and at the same time craving for that deep connection with others. He would have a deep interest in life and his own philosophical view of things. There is originality and great creativity of thought in these qualities but little chance to share them with others except perhaps through writing. His performances on the stage and on the screen epitomize his true nature. He can bring forth both the humor and the drama of his inner and outer nature through his acting. In his real life there is more drama than humor. The humor is covered over by too much seriousness due to the more serious qualities of 1, 5 and 7.

Finally, the combined names of Marlon Brando come to 5-5-1 or end with the 1 destiny number. The 5-5-1 accentuates the independent and solitary nature. The 1 in the destiny position forces him into a life of many starts. The 1 in this case compels him to become a pioneer, forever originating new projects. It has always allowed him to be his own man with the dream of having and creating something entirely his own. This 1 has moved him too far away from people. The difficulty with the 1 destiny is that it destines Marlon Brando to undertake many projects but never to see them completed, at least by his own hand. The payoff to his personal ventures never happens.

To conclude this analysis, there are some interesting changes and events that show up in the letters of his first name of Marlon.

M	A	R	L	O	N
4	5	14	17	23	28
32	33	42	45	51	56
60	61	70	73	79	84

The changes under the letters show that between the 4th and 5th, the 32nd and 33rd and the 60th and 61st birthdays there was an outstanding change, or a significant alteration in the perception of things, usually creating a greater degree of independence.

Between the 8th and 9th, the 36th and 37th and the 64th and 65th birthdays it shows some emotional difficulty that usually shows up in health problems or just a time of deep frustration.

Then between the 13th and 14th, the 41st and 42nd and the 69th and the 70th birthdays there is a time of emotional turmoil due to losses in the affections or to some tragic circumstances.

Between his 73rd and 79th birthday are some of the more stable years awakening a strong paternal response to children and family.

Those things mentioned above are not predestined, but the times indicated show tendencies only because of the intensification of certain qualities.

I have done this brief analysis of Marlon Brando to demonstrate how all of us struggle with the challenge of reconciling the many facets of our character. When we do not bring forth the highest within our qualities, the lowest will automatically express and thwart us in our endeavor to evolve mentally and spiritually.

The secret of mental growth and strength of mind lies in the knowledge of balance or the concept of mental *equilibrium.* In the early writings of the Free Masons, particularly the efforts of Albert Pike of the Scottish Rite, there is mentioned the idea of combining the two natures within us into a condition of equilibrium, which would then bring us the ultimate peace of mind. The mind with its natural concerns and responsibilities represents the outer part of the individual, while the true inward spark or unmanifest universal intelligence represents the inner aspect. The *master key* or as the Masons refer to it as the *lost word,* relates to the numbers or lessons from 1 through 9, that if incorporated into the character, will bring about that state of equilibrium between the seemingly two opposing natures. I should say that these two natures oppose each other unconsciously when there is too much conflict between the qualities within our names.

If the mind is serious in its attempt at self-inquiry it requires a tool to study itself. Problems emerge from a place of incompleteness deep within ourselves. It is not into our dysfunctional past that we need to look, but into aspects of ourselves that we are attempting to escape from. To transform ourselves we need to know how to build character and to identify the noblest part of ourselves. It is through our intelligence and our talents that we find ourselves, and through which we leave our legacy to those that follow.

In Conclusion

Up to this point you may agree that the desired or ideal way of life is to develop a substance of character that lends itself to health, happiness and success. Education from an academic standpoint is secondary to the knowledge that provides for the development and strength of character. Wisdom is the basis for power, strength and confidence. We may acquire academic credentials but never achieve much beyond a good salary. With a strong character, deep moral principles and a spiritual outlook, we can do almost anything.

For the most part I would venture to say that most people who read this book may recognize its truth but be totally incapable of applying very much of it. You may ask or wonder why so few people reach fulfillment as they near the end of their lives.

All of life is a duality. A cause and an effect. Everything we see as form or reality is the expression, or reason of something invisible that we cannot see. It is our job to feel, live and become conscious of that invisible life force or cause.

Every action produces a reaction. The reaction contains the proof and demonstrates the logic or the absence of logic of the action. All is mind. Everything is an expression of mind. The function of the mind is to become conscious of this duality and to become responsible for every action and its consequent reaction.

We are dealing with the three basic levels or states of mind, the unconscious, the conscious and the super-conscious. The unconscious mind is carried on the collective consciousness or mass mind, with little or no knowledge of what is motivating it or why things are occurring in its life. In this state the mind is compelled to deal almost exclusively with effects. The conscious mind is becoming responsible for the events occurring in its life due to the law of cause and effect, and is beginning to see and understand how it creates its own problems. The super-conscious mind has insight and deals with cause and is therefore motivated by reason or purpose. In this state the mind is detached from self or ego and is indifferent to the cares and woes of ordinary humanity.

Almost all efforts dealing with the remedial aspects of both the body and the mind have been approached through studying symptoms. This is because the symptoms are so easy to see and study. Disease for instance, is a symptom which has a root cause, but is scarcely admitted as being in the mind. Virtually all efforts to explain how the mind produces disease have fallen on deaf ears because of lack of knowledge of what the mind is, how it is created and why it expresses such levels of imbalance and its resultant tensions. Simply put, almost all disease is created through mental tension originating on a deep unconscious level. Ulcers are a good example of how worry or tension interferes with the production of acid in the stomach.

Nothing is known by the medical profession as to why everyone that worries does not suffer from ulcers or why only some people have a predisposition to ulcers. Why are certain types susceptible to specific diseases? The medical answer would be related to the genetic element, as it is passed on from one person to another. Here we are still dealing with symptoms or effects.

It is generally suspected that mind has something to do with disease but not having any knowledge of the creation of mind itself, the medical profession can do nothing else but deal with disease as they have always done.

Diet, vitamins and exercise are meager attempts that have about the same results as prescribing pills and using the scalpel. As Shakespeare has said, "Tis something, nothing." A change of lifestyle is recommended by a few who suspect the cause to be mental, but the patient can rarely change enough to make a substantial difference.

I would surely give credit where credit is due for any method used to save lives, but the next great breakthrough in medical science must be in the understanding of the basic cause of all disease as it relates to the human mind.

Psychiatry is the study of mental neurosis and the symptoms of a disturbed mind. Psychiatrists spend time categorizing and naming the many phobias in the same way that medical science deals with the physical body, naming and studying various diseases. Here again we have an attempt to isolate a seeming cause by going back into a dysfunctional childhood, and then prescribing drugs or offering counseling as the cure, with very little success. While our background, environment and parental influence are very important in explaining behavioral patterns, they cannot explain why some children coming from decent families still become sickly or disturbed mentally.

We must begin to understand the difference between the basic cause of things and a mere symptom. It is interesting to observe how two children in the same family respond to a particular experience in two totally different ways. Their response is not so much a product of their conditioning but a result of their innate nature. It is this basic or intrinsic nature that must be studied and understood. We may have two children in the same family, one is shy and sensitive, the other bold and outgoing. Why the difference? Each will respond to poor parenting in a totally different manner, and quite possibly develop phobias that correspond not only to poor parenting, but on a deeper level, to their basic mental make-up. The mind itself represents the root cause of all problems. It is demonstrated that some people can move beyond their dysfunctional backgrounds despite the hardships. Why is that? It is all related to the strength and balance of the mind through the *name.*

Your mind is comprised of every thought you have ever thought, from birth to the present moment. Your perception of life is a product of those thoughts. You are precisely the sum total of all your thoughts.

Now you are not just measured according to the number or quantity of your thoughts but also to the quality of your thinking. This is termed your character or your personality. Your personality is defined in terms of being sensitive, insensitive, introverted, extroverted, expressive, shy, soft, aggressive, practical, idealistic, restless and so on. The quality of your life could be described as leaning toward art, music, science, philosophy, business, etc. This natural inclination is not a product of your background conditioning but is a product of a definable principle which determines how you as an individual will respond to an experience. How you respond to life's experiences is due to that invisible element that we call your latent personality. What is it that determines your character type? It is language as it relates to your name.

You are a visible body as well as an invisible personality or character type. Your character develops through the quantity and quality of your thinking. You think through language. You have no consciousness without language. Other animals respond to life and their purpose according to the invisible element within themselves called instinct. The human species has a conscious function of responding to that invisible element within, through language, and through defining life and its way through conscious thought. If there is no language, there will be no consciousness. If we recall the Helen Keller story, she was deaf, blind and mute due to an illness at a very early age. She relates in her autobiography that she had absolutely no conscious awareness of anything until her nurse introduced her to language. Hence, "In the beginning was the Word, the Word was with God, and the Word was God."

Language has its intelligence through mathematics. Mathematics in its simplest form is represented through a sequence of what we call numbers (i.e., 1 is one of something, 2 is two of something, 3 is three of something, etc.). Language has its intelligence through its established sequential order (i.e., A is in the first position, B is in the second position, C in the third and so on).

Language can only be used as a medium for consciousness if the letters of any language are mathematically consistent or ordered. If the order is changed in a random fashion it would destroy its use as a medium of consciousness until the order of each letter is numerically reestablished.

It is through mathematics that language, as it is applied to the creation of mind through your *name*, creates different qualities of thought, or the differing personality traits. In the same way sound in the form of a musical scale produces the many different tones that it is made up of. It is a product of vibrational frequencies or the wave length that gives each tone its distinctiveness. Light, when passed through a prism, separates into its component colors to reveal the full color spectrum. In the same way, consciousness is separated into its component parts through language, to make up human personality and to give each person their distinctiveness and unique reason for being.

As you have learned, there are 'nine' expressions of the life force moving through language and consciousness. All of life whether it is tangible or intangible can only be understood as it takes form. We understand electricity only as it manifests as an energy to produce light, drive engines or produce a shock. Just put your finger in the socket of a light bulb and you will feel the invisible current in the form of a shock. Everything is mathematical or ordered, which determines its form and place in life, as well as giving it its meaning or reason for being. The reason of life in its most profound form through humans, is made manifest through language, thought or consciousness, and is subject to a division of nine qualities through a mathematical application.

You define yourself not so much as a certain body type, but from your personality and character or the way in which you think. You and your body respond to the forces of consciousness as they are made manifest through language and your name. You are your name. Without your name there would be no you. You would not be capable of awareness on the level of consciousness. Individuality of thought and concept would not develop. The body would grow and continue to live for a limited time but there would be no development of mind and no reason. Only the human brain is receptive to the life impulse from the realm of cause. It is through thought that the mind interprets that impulse as a conscious response, through language, which is only possible if you have a name.

You respond to the call of your name. You are identified with the forces of life as they manifest in your consciousness, through the medium of language or the letters of your name.

You will have observed the many characteristics of people that make up the human race. In this wide variety of character types, there can be observed extremes of certain traits. There are people that have the gift of the gab but never stop talking. There are people that have a penchant for detail and carry it to the extremes of fussiness. Then there are those that are quiet to the point of introversion. There are idealistic types that are impractical and those that are so practical as to lack idealism. We see business types who care for nothing but business and money, and artistic people who live exclusively for art. In some, it is not difficult to see an over-predominance or imbalance of specific qualities.

In this unbalanced state lie all the problems afflicting the human race collectively and individually. Personally it can affect our lives through poor health, broken marriages and failed businesses. Collectively we can observe it creating havoc in politics, business and religions. There are those that achieve levels of success through their efforts and those that never accomplish very much of anything, no matter how much effort they put forth. There seems to be a profound injustice in the idea of the equality of human nature. It should not be difficult to see that background and upbringing play a part in future life, but that does not explain the events of our life and the nature of our response to them.

As incredible as it may sound, the *name* reveals the whole story of one's life. It is the *balance* of the name that determines the level of initiative, the basic intelligence, the health, wealth and the entire destiny of the individual. It is the balance or imbalance of the name that determines the nature of the response to each experience.

The tension created through an unbalanced name is the product of the conflict of influences and the suppression of the positive elements therein. The body registers this tension and eventually breaks down. Through the name we can define the area or symptoms of disease that will develop in the body. All phobias and neuroses develop gradually in response to the mind's weakness or its imbalance. All success is the result of bringing forth the constructive elements and talents inherent within the name.

I will illustrate the previous ideas through a few further examples of analyses of 'first names' only. I ask the reader to keep things in perspective as they read the following analyses of people's first names. The first name is only *part* of the total picture, but it is still the most important aspect of the character and the part that is most easily recognizable. The following examples of analyses are extracted from my book, *Miracle of Names*, if you are interested in reading about yourself or your friends.

The following first names represent the dominant influence in these people's lives. I should remind you that the influences related to your month, day and year of birth, as well as the surname are also to be considered in an overall life analysis.

Margaret – Dora – Mario – Ursula –
Sonya – Moira – Lynn – Oscar

This is a deeply sensitive and impressionable quality. These people are easily influenced by their environment. Any kind of discord will affect them adversely. They have a deep yearning to be understood. They deny themselves the opportunity of being understood by being accommodating to others' needs in place of their own. Seldom do they reveal their deeper sentiments about life for fear of being misunderstood.

Their conversation is usually in support of others' ideas rather than their own, as an escape from the possibility of having their own thoughts scrutinized. They would never reveal their deeper sentiments to anyone but their closest confidant. They have a quiet and pleasant manner that is easily hurt and offended by the loud or coarse ways of others. When offended they can withdraw mentally and never show their disappointment.

This is a refined and poetic influence. They are dreamers who love to spend time alone with their books, pets and their flowers. The world of business and commerce is not for them. Their soft, quiet and easy-going disposition requires an environment of music, art and creativity. If disciplined they could excel as writers of poetry and prose, usually fiction. They are very good listeners and can divine the feelings and intentions of others. Therefore, they can offer advice that others need to hear, although they would never say anything that could hurt you.

Perseverance and hard work are not usually a strong part of their character, and they must beware of being a bit lazy and subject to bouts of procrastination. Because of their deep sensitivity and their fear of being misunderstood, they can divert the conversation away from themselves and into meaningless small-talk. This deep and private side to their nature should be cultivated and expressed along philosophical and intellectual avenues or they will be forever misunderstood.

Lacking confidence, they need encouragement, support and love, otherwise they find life a little too difficult. As women in love, they often draw the strong masculine types for support, who never understand their romantic and sensitive natures. Men of this sensitivity are drawn to the opposite sex for the safety and understanding that they do not receive from other men. They are extremely accommodating and find it difficult to say no, for fear of disappointing or witnessing the hurt feelings of anyone. They will do almost anything to avoid issues or confrontations. Being so soft and easy-going they can easily be taken advantage of. Arguments and fighting will always lead to tears and suffering. Reconciliation is always a blessed relief.

This is not a particularly healthy or robust influence, and they are quite susceptible to colds and viruses that are going around. Their physical weakness lies in the heart, lungs and bronchial organs, as well as the kidneys. Inevitably they suffer from poor circulation, with cold hands and feet. These people are idealistic, helpful and diplomatic types. Their love of nature, including animals, flowers and the tranquillity of the scene of a quiet mill pond, is the setting they require to become the artists that they are.

The imbalance in the above names makes these people oversensitive. A sadness can develop that causes them to withdraw from the mainstream of life. They tend to hide from reality by talking about sweet nothings while craving to be understood.

Kay – Pat – Dan – Ralph – Peter –
Hilary – Barry – Ira – Gillian – Ivan

These people, unlike the soft impressionable types, are independent, strong-willed and stubborn at times. This is a quality that requires its own space in order to function as a creative force, independent and free from any interference from others. As children they can be difficult to manage and to discipline because of their headstrong manner. They move towards independence early in life and strive to strike out on their own as soon as they possibly can. This is a completely honest quality, dependable and up front in everything they do and say. In their speech they are candid, and sometimes even blunt to the point where they can offend others, but not intentionally.

They have an ingenuity in figuring things out if left alone to do so. Theirs is the quality of originality. They have the perseverance and endurance to push through any obstacles that might try to stop them, and so they achieve almost anything that they put their minds to. In one sense they are appreciated by others because of their open and honest ways, but they lack the social graces and often fall short of the required diplomacy in certain situations. They can, in fact, feel out of their depth in the company of the more sophisticated and intellectual types. They would feel awkward and out of place in debates, and where they need to listen carefully to another's point of view. These people are more physically active types that do not like to spend a lot of time talking about things.

Their weakness in not being able to understand or see clearly another's point of view, makes it difficult for them to relate deeply in the more intimate matters of love and marriage. Through life, as they discover that they have difficulty relating well in relationships, there is a tendency to become more and more independent to the point of becoming somewhat unsociable. They are a little too self-oriented, and lack what is needed to function well with people on the deeper levels of communication.

Their physical weakness lies in the senses of the head, through problems affecting them in the eyes, ears, teeth, sinuses or through loss of hair. If they have injuries it is usually to their extremities – the hands, head or feet.

This is a positive and confident quality that thrives on their own initiative when focused on their own projects. They are pioneers of new ideas, but usually skeptical of anything that does not relate to things pertaining to the five senses or to their own experiences.

The imbalance in the above names produces a limitation in their mental perspective. They can only see and express life from a level based upon their own experiences exclusively. This makes them too self-oriented. They measure others' ideas too much from their own 'self' standard.

Kerry – Terry – Ned – Maureen –
Cecil – Jenny – Brent – Kent – Whitney

These people are quick-minded, clever, gutsy, ambitious and quite restless. Their versatility enables them to accomplish almost anything they put their minds to. They cannot tolerate injustice of any kind and will fight to uphold a truth. They live for the cause of truth, and are quite reactive when they are repressed or thwarted in any way. This is a very dynamic and intense quality. They must have a direction or their intensity will produce so much frustration and chaos that their lives will become impossible to live.

They are natural promoters and salespeople that will not take "no" for an answer. Life has little meaning to them if there is no challenge. They will pursue an interest as long as the challenge remains but will move on as soon as the challenge turns to routine and boredom. They cannot see that real growth is achieved through building block upon block. To them, further fields always look greener, and a change looks far more exciting than the stability that comes from consistent effort and following things through to completion.

Their lives are a series of experiences with a great deal learned at a cost. One thing that forever eludes them is happiness and peace of mind. They can never relax, except for short periods of time, and usually only after some great physical exertion. They are versatile and their love of freedom is the essence of their being. Their fierce independence and restlessness make it difficult for them in relationships. At times they can be quite critical, and know just what to say that hurts, but they find it very hard to take criticism themselves.

When focused they can achieved almost the impossible. They have an insatiable urge for discovery and new things. They love the idea of change and travel. They can be disruptive and radical in their outlook on life, and respond from the gut level to anything that smacks of an untruth. There is nothing they won't try, once their interest is awakened. They have a touch of the daredevil and could become great gamblers.

They are driven by their intensity to succeed, but when depressed, they are prey to some very destructive thoughts towards themselves. They never forget a slight against themselves, and must curb the urge to get even.

Their weakness lies in their solar plexus and their stomach. They are prone to ulcers and other stomach upsets. Tension will also affect them in the muscles around the shoulders and neck.

Sleep can be impossible when they become worked up mentally.

When these people are motivated by a cause of justice or truth, they can move mountains. It is their purpose to use their mind and intellect to sift through the old outworn dogmas, and to uncover the truths of life that others lack the courage to pursue.

The above names suffer in their imbalance through feeling constantly driven. Peace of mind and stability for the most part are non-existent. The mental intensity makes it difficult for these people to live with others or to live with themselves, unless they have a great deal of variety and creativity in their daily lives.

Rose – Joe – Graham – Sandra –
Anna – Sara – Owen – Leroy – Charlene

As children these people are happy, energetic, playful and loving. They love to tease and have fun, and never take life too seriously, and this character trait carries on throughout their lives. They have the gift of the gab, and at times they can get carried away with it. They are artistic and creative, but quite scattered in their efforts and seldom finish the things they start. They are warm, friendly and outgoing to everyone, and are strongly drawn to the opposite sex.

This is a soft, loving and impressionable quality that requires encouragement, support and a strong helping hand if they are to have any degree of success in their lives. Lacking in self-discipline they must be careful that they are not influenced and drawn into the association of those who would mislead them. When disciplined into such fields as dancing, music or public speaking they can excel. They could make fine entertainers. If they find themselves doing mundane or routine types of work, they become restless, unhappy and unreliable workers.

This is a quality that is not suited to heavy physical labor or to anything which requires hard work. They have a sensitivity to the feelings of others. They work best in association with others, where they can help and interact on a fun and happy level. Being emotional types, they thrive on and are motivated through inspiration, but due to the lack of concentration and staying power, they most often fail to persevere in their endeavors. In their interaction with others, their accommodating natures allow them to flow into conversation with almost anyone. Their speech is so fluid, that at times they can hardly stop it. They love debating but are easily drawn into arguments. Being social types they must be careful about their conversations regarding other people. They love to talk about others. This is not a deep or philosophical influence.

Physically, they are susceptible to problems affecting them in the kidneys, liver or the bloodstream. They must learn to stay away from too many sweet foods, or they can be affected through diabetes and other blood diseases.

They are also prone to poor circulation and swollen ankles later on in life. This is an affectionate, intuitive and feeling quality that depends on and works well with others. Lacking independence and individuality, these people need the proper direction and guidance if they are to succeed in life. Because of their emotional natures, if they are not disciplined and directed into artistic fields, they can become indulgent in their physical appetites. Their creative potential knows no bounds, but if misdirected they can become lazy and influenced by life in the fast lane.

The imbalance in the above names produces a sense of irresponsibility, and a carefree attitude that inevitably leads to indulgence in many forms through lack of discipline.

So it is then that we respond to life's experiences from our innate quality of character or mind. How we respond to our environment is directly due to the basic nature of our mind as it is created through language and the name. If the mind is unbalanced to begin with, its response to life will eventually become distorted and produce the many phobias we see in the lives of people. Everything lies in balance. In the same way, music is merely sound based upon harmonics produced through combining relative tones or notes.

The mind is just a correlation of mental forces or qualities, and when they are not correlated properly they respond to an experience to produce distortion, in the same way that combining notes of music that are not harmonious, creates a discord.

If we are to transcend the problematic states of mind we must study mind in all its component parts. Transcendence refers to the idea of going beyond the present state into a higher one. In a spiritual sense it means drastically altering the mental state to where it is no longer problematic.

With an unbalanced mind it is impossible to transcend its problems. The problem dictates the nature of its thoughts and controls the mind and keeps it a prisoner, confined to a specific level or plane of thought.

With a balanced mind a person can change their plane of thought and adapt to new circumstances, and therefore alter the actual state of their thinking. Balance gives the potential for versatility and mental focus. Balance provides strength, confidence and initiative. We must be capable of succeeding at our goals and aspirations in order to understand their value and the lessons that they can teach us. Success in our personal ambitions must precede the transcendent process. If failure in our personal life produces an excuse and an escape into so-called spiritual interests, the motive force is usually a form of ego that makes the entrance on the spiritual path virtually impossible. Unbalanced thinking produces an emotional condition where the thinking revolves endlessly around objects of unconscious origins.

We can only transcend with our mind through our thinking. Most of us I dare say cannot think. Thinking requires concentration and vital force or energy. The mind receives or creates thought through focus. Mind is either entirely influenced by vagrant thought forces or it has become a master of thought and is capable of insight.

The transcendent mind recognizes mental interference or useless and destructive thoughts as uncontrollable images due to an emotional condition. All problems originate in this plane of mind.

Dabbling in spiritual ideas through exercises, psychic phenomena and over-sensitivity are ways of enhancing one's imagination and producing an exalted state of egotism through mysticism.

Energy

Energy is of a mental origin. It cannot be manipulated or created through diet, vitamins or other food substances. Proper food is necessary to keep the body healthy and fit as an instrument for consciousness and the mental force. Energy is the substance of life itself. Energy could be considered the current of life or the spirit force that comes into the body with the first breath, and is thereafter sustained by the breath. It only seems that good food or concentrated food substances create energy, when really they only provide nourishment to the body so that the energy or mental force can be felt as a feeling of vitality. If the mind is balanced, a simple diet of vegetables, fruits and grains are all that are necessary to maintain a healthy body. Stimulating food substances act upon the body to produce the sensation of energy or a 'high' that the mind cannot control and the result is a letdown or 'low.'

Energy or the life current is dependent upon 'vital force' which is carried and maintained through the bloodstream. All aspects of mind, thought and memory depend upon this vital force. If it is absent, concentration becomes impossible and the mind becomes a prey to emotional or vagrant thought forms or images. If the instrument or body degenerates too far, then senility occurs where the mind and memory cannot express clearly. It might be interesting to note that the mind, in the senile state, actually remains fully intact but can no longer express itself through a worn-out body devoid of vital force.

Creative thought requires vital force, and vital force is maintained through a balanced mind and a stable emotional nature. Any form of emotional indulgence depletes the vital force through over-stimulation of the nervous system. When this occurs, the mind loses its ability to maintain an even keel. Suddenly the mind becomes either moody, irritable or suffers depressions and fears over the most trivial matters. It blames and criticizes without recognizing that it has lost control of its thinking. At a certain point when the vital force is built up again, the mind regains its stability and its power to be kind, tolerant and understanding. Worry keeps the average mind in a perpetual state of fear and physical depletion, so that the person swings from happiness to unhappiness without ever knowing why.

The lesson relating to *'the conservation of the vital force'* is a most profound one. As the mind evolves to higher and higher states, it becomes aware of the slightest deviation in thought that could lead to a depletion of the vital force. In this higher state the mind becomes aware of the difference between emotional thinking and creative thought.

Sexual stimulation has a profound effect upon the vital force through the nervous system. This vital force can be quickly depleted through over-stimulation of the nervous system during arousal. A conscious mind is aware of the agitation registering through the nerves at the time of arousal, and should be able to direct the awakened spiritual force beyond the agitation for the purpose of deep relaxation. Because the spiritual force has been awakened through the physical channel, in most cases there will be a depletion of the vital force. This depletion may register immediately or it may not occur for a few days depending on the nature of the connection between the couple. The effect with most people will be a swing in one's mood.

I have gradually come to know that virtually any disease of the body can be cured if the body can maintain its vital force. This is not a simple procedure and can only be done when the mind understands how to live in the absence of mental tension. Every wrong thought, concept and theory has the effect of producing tension, and results in burning up the vital force in the blood stream. Truly, our ignorance of the principles of life is no excuse for our suffering. The ultimate solution lies in creating balance out of imbalance.

As the mind becomes more conscious, it becomes aware of the effects of emotionally stimulating experiences and how they work through the nervous system to deplete the vital force. Most emotionally stimulating experiences become habitual and addictive. They bring a sense of pleasure which is actually artificial. At this point the mind becomes trapped in illusion, or as they say in the East, confounded by 'Maya.' When we become dependent on pleasure, the mind loses its power and its creativity. At this stage we have become 'sense dependent.' Now the mind is impressed with images and thoughts that are not real. At this point the mind can no longer discriminate between what is real and that which is illusory.

The ego or 'self' is spawned and grows through and around this illusion. When the mind is caught in this scenario it is compelled to live in and for emotional stimulation. This kind of life represents the roller-coaster existence that mankind is generally living. Indulgence in TV, sex, loud music, mysticism, religious revivals and 'new age' fantasies are the thrills that keep the mass of people stimulated and addicted to their egos. This is the stuff that keeps people worked up, their nervous systems jangled and their vital force exhausted.

If any one of these people chooses to step off the treadmill, the first reaction will be to suffer symptoms of withdrawal. It is only the strong that can commit to the higher path. Becoming religious is not enough. Developing a simple morality is only the beginning.

The incentive to move beyond emotionalism or sense dependence must come from the soul itself. There must be a sensing that a transcendent state even exists. This transcendent state requires a transformation into a spiritual morality that is beyond the capacity of common religion. Common religion is still steeped in emotionalism, sympathy and sentimentality.

Energy is the very current of life itself as it expresses through a creative mind, directed with purpose toward spiritual evolution. Emotionalism is an escape and an avoidance of reality. This leads to retrogression, sadness, self-pity and disease.

Emotion

We could say that emotion is the very life current itself expressing through the body in a wide spectrum of feeling that gives life its substance or form. Nothing is real except through sensation as it operates through the senses.

We cannot move beyond emotion while we are living and experiencing life. Without emotion we are dead. The spirit force requires the body, and through emotion it makes contact on the finite plane through sensation.

Virtually all of our life experiences are felt as sensations or feelings of sadness, grief, pain, joy, exhilaration, etc.

The mind is the directive force and determines the nature of the sensation and its outcome. The emotions register or reflect every thought as well as the general state of mind. It can be a feeling of well-being or a continued state of worry. In any case, how we feel at any moment exactly corresponds to how we are thinking and what we are thinking.

Now it is interesting to note that when ego is present in one's thinking, the effect through the emotions works through the nervous system to produce agitation and depletion of the vital force. For example, public speaking or performing can produce nervousness which is just a form of self-concern or ego that is very exhausting. Over-excitement of any kind is usually a play of the ego and results in depletion. If ego is present in any aspect of sensation there will be an agitation felt through the nervous system. Any form of ego gratification produces a similar reaction in the nervous system.

As the mind grows to experience a more selfless state, the power of life or emotion begins to express without distortion upon the nervous system. The mind is no longer in reaction to the play of ego and cannot be influenced, and is therefore in control of the nervous system. An agitated nervous system can never be construed as joy or happiness. Music for instance can either be used to bring happiness and relaxation, or it can be used to excite the emotions. Whether music is good or destructive depends upon what aspect of the mind and its interests it feeds. If it feeds something evil within the mind it will still register a feeling of excitement, although, in the latter case the effect upon the emotions and nervous system will create depletion, as well as leading the mind astray.

Eventually our mind must raise itself high enough so that it awakens feelings and sensations that vibrate within the body and nervous system without agitation. All things can be enjoyed without fear of negative consequences when we are able to discriminate between good and bad.

The mind at this point is not distorted and therefore cannot register any distortion through the nervous system. The mind can now reflect the power of life or emotion freely through the senses. It is possible then to experience an expanded awareness or feeling for what is reality. At this point there is no over-excitement, only peace and calm. This is not to say that we shouldn't have fun and experience excitement. It is a matter of quality and degree.

Self-inquiry should be used as an exercise in analyzing the effects of our own thoughts as they register through our emotions. Wrong or selfish thoughts and imperfect concepts of life leave impressions in the emotions that create feelings that are mildly or deeply disturbing. The tensions that most people suffer lie below the level of their consciousness because they have not practiced the art of self-inquiry. These tensions can disturb or agitate the nervous system just enough to make us continually unhappy. With the average person, their escape from this unhappiness is through further indulgence in emotionally stimulating experiences which have the effect of perpetuating the dilemma.

The emotions give power and form to our thoughts through sensation. The mind can only be analyzed through its effect on the emotions. Ego is that element of the mind that distorts. It is self-serving and must be detected and flushed out as it leaves its impression upon the emotions and the nervous system. This requires honesty, concentrated analysis and a basis in a philosophy as large as life itself.

Breathing

Breath is the active ingredient of the body, and supplies and sustains the mind with the power to think. I venture to say that the run of humanity have never truly exercised the power to think. The nature of our thoughts draws things to itself accordingly. Thinking is the only way to resolve anything. The problematic state can only be transcended through right thinking. How we feel reflects precisely how we think.

Thinking is more difficult than we may imagine. It requires focus, concentration and above all, vital force. If we have no purpose to our life, continuity of thought is impossible. We must awaken the passion for life by subduing the obsessive passion for useless pursuits that drain the energies. As we pursue a goal that is useful to ourselves and others, eventually the spirit or passion is awakened, but not until long years have been spent in the development and refinement of that goal. Only then is the mind charged with energy and purpose.

The breath we breathe is by far the greatest source of vital force. The time we live in is heavy with the struggle to survive, and the mind is pulled into countless avenues of distraction. This preoccupation with distractions produce the struggle between the two natures within us, the higher and the lower, each one competing for control.

There is great power in the breath as many have discovered, particularly those in the East. Breathing exercises are vital but should be practiced with a full awareness of all the consequences.

You might ask why additional breathing is necessary? Because unless we have an environment of harmony and peace, in a society where there is no tensions or pressures, we do not have enough motive force to push past the mass or collective fear which unconsciously holds people in conformity. Only when the mind is free of this mass influence can it think clearly. The average mind I dare say is not in control of its own thoughts. It lives in a sea of thought impressions, not of its own making, and is pulled into thoughts shared by the mass of people that have no purpose. We could call this emotional thinking influenced by the desire for sense stimulation. So many theories promulgated through books and the media encourage a widespread interest in life from a sensual perspective.

The sexual revolution in the past several decades is an example of how thoughts are perpetuated to keep sensuality alive and the mind preoccupied, if only on a level that is mostly unconscious. Most minds are unconscious of the mental bombardment of thoughts because of a dream-like mental state. Pursuing our desires endlessly with little success opens the mind to this dreamy state. Only when these desires are gratified do we stop the agony, but only for a brief moment, then shortly after we discover that we are still not happy. We then find new desires that put us back on the treadmill. Desire is not wrong but to live constantly in that desire state is obsessive. Our egos thrive and perpetuate themselves through our desire nature. Desire is necessary. It is a motive force in life but destructive if the mind cannot think. It is the purpose of the mind to use desire to initiate thought and not to be controlled by it. If the mind and its power to think have never been developed, then theories that suggest we put it aside as an interference seem plausible but insidious.

If the power in the breath is properly directed, the mind can free itself from this heavy plane of inertia, and experience lightness and the ability to discriminate between useless thought and creative insight. This activity is not passive as in meditation but is active and relaxing.

Let us not presume that a few breathing exercises will transport you to the lofty climes of success. In fact, to begin with, life usually becomes more intense at the outset of increased breathing.

Breathing adds power to thought and feeling. This is why in the ancient Indian philosophy it was not encouraged unless there was balance and mental maturity. Breathing will accelerate the growth process, but only if the mind can become conscious of what is happening. Increased breathing initially intensifies all thought forms, good and bad. If you do not have sufficient individuality you must be careful in pursuing breathing exercises. The increased breathing is not designed to make you feel good but to make or allow you to think. At times there may be a feeling of increased energy. A momentary feeling of happiness may be the result of the exercise but that is not the objective. It is only at a certain advanced point that the mind will feel sure and confident about its own thoughts, and then avoid the compulsive urge to pursue thoughts of worry, fear or criticism. Do not expect success too quickly.

Begin the exercise by sitting in a comfortable chair and taking about six deep, quick breaths through the mouth. End the final breath by expelling the air and holding it out for fifteen to thirty seconds, while completely relaxing. It is in the holding out of the breath that the mind can quickly induce complete relaxation. While holding the breath out you may either close or keep your eyes open. Then take a deep breath through the nose and hold it in as long as you feel like. Then start again at the beginning. If you are doing these exercises correctly you will feel exhilarated. Become aware of how you feel and if there are any disturbing sensations or thoughts. Stop the breathing if there is an increased feeling of mental negativity or emotional intensity.

Use the increased power of your breath to focus on positive and happy thoughts. Refuse to let negative thoughts use you. The object is to move past all vagrant thought forms and negative images and feelings. After a time you should feel truly amazed at the focus achieved to solve problems in the light of clear thinking. The exercise should only take between five to ten minutes depending on how quickly you can bring your mind to a complete state of relaxation.. The length of time for this exercise is purely an individual matter. Do this exercise throughout the day as often as you feel the need. Never overdo it.

There are many variations to these exercises, and each person should find the form that best suits them and their disposition, as well as their level of growth. There are many other breathing exercises which can produce very interesting effects on the mind but that is not the subject of these pages.

"Many are called but few are chosen."

This statement suggests that the very soul of some individuals compels them to search out the way of spirituality from a point of necessity or destiny rather than from desire or idealism. They are first motivated to search due to personal suffering and eventually they draw their incentive from within through an awakened sense of purpose and their destiny.

Everyone is called and everyone suffers, but the majority who suffer are pulled into the realm of self-pity and blame. The vast majority of would-be seekers are confounded by the perpetual question, "Where am I going?" Those that are chosen know where they are going at a fairly early age. They cannot be stopped. It is for these few to leave a record of their thoughts for those that follow. Nothing is predestined. Life is a process of expansion or evolution. Consciousness is the realization of this process. Destiny is awakened through the realization of the inner quality of our mind. Individuality frees us to explore the universality and relativity of all things.

Perhaps the 'soul' provides the urge and prompts the mind into action. In any case the mind must understand the process of mental development if there is going to be any soul growth. Happiness is not a result of many incarnations of the soul or spark of life. Happiness is everyone's birthright in every life if we presume to accept the re-incarnation theory. Life was never meant to be a continual struggle. It is only ignorance of the principles of life that perpetuates the struggle from one age to the next. It is not a matter of evolution in this case. It is simply a matter of education.

As children, most of us experienced exceedingly happy times. A child's senses are clear and open to the beauty of life. I personally appreciated nature and things as deeply then as I do now. This did not require great effort or training. It does not require many lifetimes to be happy. Happiness is inherent and present within every child.

The cloud that later moved over my life as it does for almost everyone, was the cloud of misinformation and the absence of the simple truths of life. Simple truth has been withheld as well as being misconstrued. Like so many others, I gradually and systematically became educated to deal with and endure the struggle to maintain a living with the unspoken promise, which was never explained, that the future would open up with untold happiness. Another illusion! I wasted my time struggling when I should have been developing my true potential. Fortunately for me those years of struggle did build character and a certain awareness of the futility of a life without a purpose.

What are the few great souls 'chosen' for? Simply to add their substance and their talents to life for the benefit of others and to be an example of exemplary conduct and a revelator of truth as it unfolds through their morality and love of life.

Religions of today have a huge responsibility to keep up with the times and to sift out the dogma that is not relevant or useful to spiritual evolution. The promise of salvation or enlightenment, through methods of belief in rituals or spiritual practices, can never be replaced by good sound logic and the understanding of the ultimate wisdom behind life. In our desperation we turn to and rely upon mystical theories that promise relief from our agonies, only because we have not been able to awaken the powers of thought.

Throughout history new religious perceptions develop out of the efforts of great minds who challenge and *protest* existing dogmas that have led to practices in idolatry. The old is replaced by the new and it isn't long before the new succumbs to the same fate or fatalism as the old. The idea that we need to worship and rely upon our gods for the solution to our problems seeps into our consciousness through self-pity and desperation and leaves us without trust in our own powers. We may pray for peace and wait for an eternity for its deliverance and never take a meaning from the exercise. A prayer is futile when it causes us to wait for a reply. Every thought, good or bad, is like a prayer whose value lies in action and follow-through. If an entreaty to the gods for an answer to our problems replaces mental inquiry, we only stay the progress of reason and then perpetuate the problem.

If meditation is an excuse to escape from contemplation it will only succeed in putting the mind to sleep. Relaxation and mental peace come through finding solutions to problems. Meditation is a mental condition of reception achieved after the mind has used the power of concentration and inquiry. Meditation occurs naturally within a happy and inquiring mind. If meditation is used to induce relaxation, the habit can obscure the reason for the stress or tension in the first place. For certain types of minds, meditation can be an escape from the need to think, which can then lead the mind to a condition of over-sensitivity. To use an image of God as the focus for meditation, in expectation of God-realization, is the height of egotism and an escape from the real work. If the object of meditation is to bring forth the *highest* within ourselves, we must first bring our mind, through concept, to that high place. Meditation will never dissipate vagrant thought forms, phantoms and useless images that emerge spontaneously. Worry, fear and any unresolved issues in our life produce their relative images and phantoms. Only as the mind awakens to the wisdom of life, will the mind relax spontaneously into a meditative state devoid of mental interferences.

The question is, can the mind make contact with the solutions to its own problems? Of course it can but only if it begins its inquiry from the basis of a logical theory of life.

Throughout this discourse I have often used the term 'fatalism' as a trap that humanity has fallen into because life seems so awfully difficult to sort out by ourselves. We have set up gods and systems and exercises designed to help us get through life with the hope that God as an intermediary, can be appealed to in our moments of despair and anguish. In this state of expectation lies the source of all our problems and the perpetuation of our misery. Behind the veil between life and death there is no one answering our prayers. We are bound to our problematic states through our self-centered and egotistical perceptions. We set up our gods in our own images so that we can, in our imagination, carry out a conversation with them, and make our appeals and express our complaints. It only serves to bind us to our gods in hope, expectation and defeat. It is only when we are strong enough that we can sever the connection with objects of worship and personality and so discover our true divine natures. The mind itself is capable of self-revelation, but only when it can move itself beyond fear and self-pity and *not* cry out. God the reason, being beyond personality, neither punishes nor rewards. It is up to us to understand the way of life and the operation of thought, desire, good and evil and the laws of cause and effect. There is nothing so releasing and enlightening as that confidence that comes when we know that we are a free spirit, bound only by our own ignorance and any fear of God. All great minds experience the essence of life, and at times are overwhelmed and humbled by the grandness of the scheme of things and the spirit which is embodied in life and living. It has been my inspiration to outline in this treatise a mere implication of what lies ahead for anyone who takes up the study of this profound work.

Time

Time and growth are relative terms, and both exist because of *purpose.* The master key that unlocks the mystery of life relates to self-discovery and purpose. We only have so much time to come to fulfillment, or we will be left behind hanging on in vain to our last breath, totally unaware of the reason for our existence.

To come to fulfillment is to know the reason for our life. Unhappiness cannot exist when the mind comes into self-realization. Our entire life must be committed to something useful. Not a moment in time should be wasted in worry. All problems exist through worry or a life without purpose. Time either sees life moving forward or backward, but never standing still. Happiness is a concept that will not accept worry as a necessary part of progress because worry denies the existence of purpose. To sustain the feeling of well-being is simply a matter of having confidence in the existence of your own divine spark which is timeless. That divine spark individualized is nothing less than life itself as it evolves through time and human experience. If the mind is to survive it must apply purpose to itself in order to see and experience the beauty of life.

It is worth further emphasis of these points because there is a message here that should not be missed. Remember that *only* the seed that produced the *flower* can perpetuate itself through the production of the new seed. Only in the flowering of our effort can there be a continuation of life, or of the soul.

APPLICATION FOR A PERSONAL ANALYSIS OF YOUR NAME

The simplest way of demonstrating the truth of the underlying principles of this work is through providing you with a personal life analysis. You will not be able to deny the accuracy of the analysis. It is well to remember that few people in life reach levels of personal fulfillment. Why is this? It is because their names are unbalanced. In the analysis you will be shown how your mind responds to your life experiences to either thwart your deepest desires, or if you are fortunate to have a balanced name, your response will more easily move you to reach your goals. You will clearly see that most of us are too one-sided in the make-up of our personality, and this imbalance inhibits the natural expression of our true spiritual nature. Some of us talk too much, or too little. Others lean too heavily towards the practical side of life, while others live in a dream world. Then there are those who have great confidence and those who suffer terribly from lack of confidence. All of these character traits and idiosyncrasies will be described in the analysis and much more. The first part of the analysis will describe your true inner nature and the best direction to take when choosing occupations and personal interests. The main objective is to show you why you may not be able to reach your life objectives and what you can do about it. There is no doubt that the analysis will open your mind to an awareness of yourself that will amaze you. This is not a vain promise but an actual fact. The analysis in itself is not going to transform your life, but if you perceive its deeper implication it could transform the way you eventually look at life itself and those around you.

For an Analysis of Your Life Send the Following Information:

Full Legal Name: ____________________

Gender *[male or female]*: ____________________

Maiden Name: ____________________

Name Most Used: ____________________

Business Signature *[please print]*: ____________________

Birthdate *[month – day – year]*: ____________________

Time of Birth *[if near midnight]*: ____________________

Address *[including Zip or Postal Code]*:

____

____

Phone Number: ____________________

Cost: $65 US or $80 CAN
It will be done on a 90-minute audio cassette.

Mail this information to:
Clayne Conings
123 North Holdom
Burnaby BC Canada
V5B 1K2

For information on courses write to the above address, phone 604/299-2337, email *guiding@intergate.ca* or visit our website at *www.miracleofnames.com*

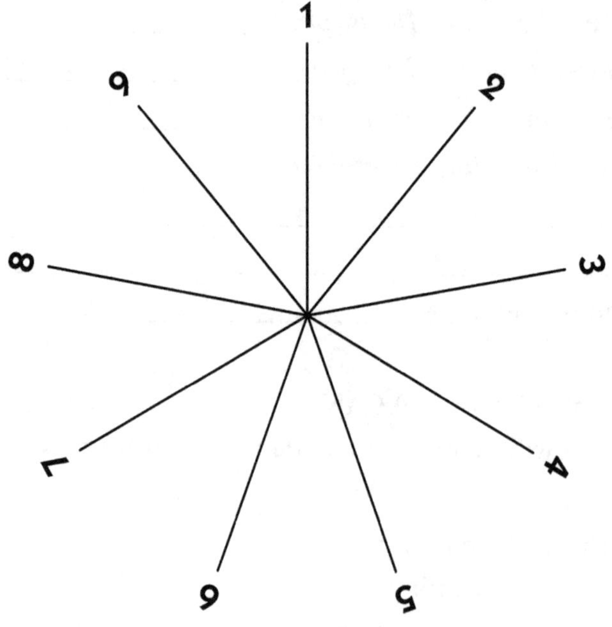
1
2
3
4
5
6
7
8
9

CPSIA information can be obtained
at www.ICGtesting.com
Printed in the USA
LVHW111213100120
643149LV00001B/4/P